GOALS DO COME TRUE

From The Edge Of Financial Oblivion To A Life Of Freedom & Fun

By Doug Bennett

ISBN: 9798559309712
Imprint: Independently published

Copyright 2020, Doug Bennett

This book was produced in collaboration with Write Business Results Limited. For more information on their business book, blog and podcast services, please visit www.writebusinessresults.com or contact the team via info@writebusinessresults.com.

Contents

Contents

Acknowledgements

My mum, Lucy Bennett – stolen from my brother Jim's tattoo, 'Your strength will guide me always.'

David Braithwaite – if you lived an hour, or two hours, further on, I would still have offered you a lift.

Michelle Hoskin – if you want your butt kicked, there is no one better! Only took me three years to sack Bonnie. I am a slow learner.

MDRT 'the usual suspects' – thanks for your continued support, banter and love.

My greater MDRT family – if you are in the financial services industry and want to turn your life around, aim to qualify for MDRT, The Premier Association of Financial Professionals®. You will not regret it. There are so many to thank, so if you are in MDRT and our paths have crossed and we shared a moment, lunch, dinner, a seminar, a beer or most importantly an idea, then I thank you!

Dan Sullivan and the Strategic Coach® Program – especially Julie Cosgrave, for introducing me and gently nudging me along for I don't know how many years. I hope you finally got credit for me joining! If you didn't then at least everyone who reads this book will know it's because of you that I joined the Program. Although towards the end it was feeling like a rather expensive quarterly get-together (the result of my very low follow-through), there is so much I can track back to either receiving first-hand or being reminded of that has contributed to my success.

Paul Armson and Inspiring Advisers Online – Paul provides support for advisers to take their business from purely transactional to providing a tangible service. Paul provided me with the missing piece of the jigsaw for my business and gave me confidence to talk to clients with considerably more money. I was already confident in the £50,000–£200,000 space, but now I understand that, to quote Tony Gordon, 'Bigger is not more complicated, bigger is just bigger', and I am confident with clients of all sizes.

Acknowledgements

Legends of Wisdom – Brian Tracy, Tom Hopkins, Jim Rohn, Jack Canfield, Norman Vincent Peale, Tony Gordon and Dale Carnegie, and the new kids on the block Simon Sinek and Tim Ferriss.

My team – thanks for everything you do to make me look great. Full training will be given!!!

Big thanks to Georgia Kirke and the Write Business Results team for helping me to bring this book to life.

My sons Jason and Jake – you make me so very proud!

Bonnie – many promises have been made throughout our time together, I can now finally come good on all of them. Just let me have the revised list and let me know in what order you would like the list completed. I love you.

Foreword

Michelle Hoskin

I've spent over 20 years working alongside some of the world's most successful financial services firms. I'm a speaker, a coach, a mentor and I design international best practice standards of operational excellence. I know a lot of people in the financial services sector and I can honestly tell you that there aren't many like Doug.

One of the first things I realised about him was that he's a lovely guy whom I'd describe as being squidgy in the centre. I can't think of any better way to describe his gentleness and kindness.

We first met at an MDRT meeting in Atlanta in 2011. I remember that he showed me a photo of his wife, Bonnie, and I replied, 'Bloody hell, you're punching above your weight aren't you?' That set the tone for our friendship. I'm very honest and straight talking (as you might have guessed). A few days later, Doug and I both found ourselves with some free time, so we hit the pool.

I distinctly remember that one of the first conversations we had that day involved me telling him that he needed to fire Bonnie from his business. I could see that he was stranded without any real direction at that point, so I held up a mirror to his face and told him exactly how things were and how things weren't.

I've seen how he has upped the ante and worked hard to grow his business. I've watched him grow in confidence, and helped him along the way. One of the phrases I learned from Doug is, 'Success leaves clues.' He embraced the idea that you become the average of the five people you spend the most time with and surrounded himself with people who were incredibly successful. I also saw the flipside of this, when he was trying to emulate those around him instead of focusing on what he truly wanted, and I helped him realise that he didn't need a massive business with 15 members of staff to be successful. I was also the person who encouraged Doug to start speaking on stage.

Throughout all the challenges he's faced and the success he's gained, one thing has remained the same, and that's Doug. As a person, he hasn't changed. He's still the man I met in Atlanta, who is kind, gentle and squidgy in the middle. He hasn't forgotten where he came from, or who has helped him along the way. Doug has stayed true to himself. He's taken his time, worked his way up steadily and thought about what he's doing.

And now we come to the reason that you're reading my foreword – this book. Doug wants to help people, it's in his nature. He has a heart of gold and always thinks of others before himself. He's genuine in how he lives his life, and he has a genuine desire to help you improve your business. That's what this book is all about. It's his way of reaching out to and helping even more people.

If you need another reason to read this book from cover to cover, it's that Doug is genuine. There are very few people who, despite their success, remain squidgy in the centre, but Doug has; and that's why you should read this book. He isn't motivated by anything other than a genuine intention of doing good, so learn what you can from his experiences. I certainly believe that we could all benefit from being more like Doug.

Michelle Hoskin, aka Little Miss WOWW!®, Founder and Director of Standards International

Preface

David Braithwaite

There are certain people in your life who make you feel better after having been in their company. Doug is one of those people.

Having known Doug for over ten years, I can confidently say that he's written this book because he genuinely wants to help you, the reader, improve your business and achieve your potential. I first met Doug when he came to speak to a group of advisers I was part of. We've all met people whom we can instantly relate to, and that was exactly how it was the first time I heard Doug speak. During that presentation, he showed me what was possible and introduced me to a world of financial advising and mortgage protection advice that was outside what I'd experienced up until that point.

Meeting Doug that day inspired me to do more than I had before, and showed me that I could achieve more than I'd thought possible. In the years that have followed, Doug has been not only an inspiration in the business world, but also a good friend.

We are both MDRT members and it was at the MDRT conference in Atlanta in 2011 where we became firm friends. During that trip, Doug opened up to me about the challenges he was facing and we both realised that we needed to rediscover our mojo, so to speak. Since then, we've been good friends and both found our passion for our work.

If you haven't yet had the pleasure of meeting Doug Bennett I can tell you now that he's a very inspiring person. This book might be about business success, but unlike others that you might have read before, Doug's journey has been anything other than smooth. In fact, I'd describe it like a scenic railway journey. I know that there have been times in the past when he's thought about packing it all in and giving up. But he never did. He persevered.

I'll let him tell his story in the following pages, because he speaks from the heart and you'll realise that finding success isn't always easy and hasn't always been easy for Doug. One thing I can tell you is that no matter what is going on in his life, Doug always has a smile and is always happy to help. I'd go so far as to say that he'll go out of his way to help anybody, even when he maybe shouldn't.

That said, I can think of more than one occasion when he's helped me. One particular story sticks in my mind. Three years ago, I broke my leg and couldn't leave the house for months. The first time I ventured out was to go to an MDRT meeting in London. Getting around London with a leg in a cast on crutches was no mean feat. Doug was with me and helped me by carrying my bag and so on. By the end of the day, I was exhausted.

The next day, Doug and I were both going to a conference in Birmingham. I only just made the train and it wasn't a pleasant journey. I made it to the conference though and once the day had finished, we all headed to the bar for a drink. I was still standing up, on my crutches, but I was exhausted by this point and I was in agony. Doug disappeared to find me a chair so that I could sit down before I fell over. We were both staying the night and the next morning we met for breakfast. My leg was still incredibly sore, my foot had swollen up and I was dreading the thought of getting the train home.

While we were having breakfast, Doug said the best thing he's ever said to me. He asked, 'Would you like a lift home?' The thought was heaven. Although Doug and I don't live far from each other, my house is half an hour further on from his, so he added an hour to his journey, which was already about 2.5 hours long, just to drop me off at my door when I'm sure that all he wanted to do was get home to Bonnie.

Doug didn't hesitate to offer me a lift and that's just one of many examples I could give you of how Doug does whatever he can to make other people happy. He'll go out of his way to help you, which is why I know he will be so thrilled that you're reading this book and able to learn from his challenges and successes.

Doug has been through a lot in his life and I couldn't be happier that he's achieved the success that he has. I can't think of anyone else who is more deserving of success and happiness. It means a lot to me that he's shared his journey with me and wants me to be along for the ride. I hope that you enjoy the ride as much as I have.

David Braithwaite, Founder and Director of Citrus Financial Management Ltd

Introduction

The inspiration for this book came from a list of goals that I'd written years ago and forgotten about. I rewrote my goals over the years with an occasional date. My first set of goals was written in 2004 and included completing the London Marathon, which I achieved in 2005. When I found this list of goals in 2012, I was amazed to see that I'd achieved nearly all of them.

These goals were related to my business and my personal life. As we go through the book I'll share some of them with you and give you advice on how I achieved them. Sometimes I didn't even realise that what I was doing at the time was leading me towards another of my goals. But looking back I've realised how everything connects.

My journey isn't a linear one. I've had success and failure along the way. In fact, just a decade ago I was on the edge of bankruptcy and now I'm a millionaire. Consistently setting goals has been instrumental in helping me get to where I am today, with a successful business, a healthy bank balance and, most importantly, a happy marriage.

There are also certain core values that I believe are essential in the financial advice profession, although they are equally applicable in any business. In fact, many of the ideas you'll find in this book will lend themselves to any new business. If you cultivate these, you'll not only find that you are happier in yourself but also that you develop a loyal client base who will stay with you through thick and thin.

Throughout the book I talk about my wonderful wife, Bonnie. I've written this from a personal perspective, so wherever you see the word 'wife', feel free to interpret this as husband/spouse/significant other – whatever term you choose.

If you're just starting out in the world of financial services and have ambitions of running your own business, the advice I provide in this book will certainly help you set off on your journey on the right foot. If you already have a business, I hope that this book will help reinvigorate your passion for your work and give you some useful advice that improves your business' performance, whether you're currently doing well or have hit a rough patch.

More than anything, I hope that this book helps you to create a happy and balanced life. Working hard is all well and good, but if it's to the detriment of your personal life then what's the point? I hope that sharing my journey and some of the mistakes that I've made along the way will help you to avoid a few of the same traps and give you a smoother path to success.

I have more than 30 years of experience in financial services. I've had professional triumphs and faced professional challenges. I've been through some very challenging personal times too. But I've come out the other side with a smile on my face and I'm happy to say that I've achieved the success I always wanted. I'm proof that goals do come true, so join me as we explore what you can do to make sure your goals come true too.

Chapter 1: No Diving Allowed

Financial simplicity

I'd like you to imagine that you're visiting the beach for the very first time. You're sitting on the sand, listening to the waves crashing onto the beach, enjoying the sunshine. Because it's really sunny, you keep applying suntan lotion throughout the day. At some point you feel as though you need to cool off. Remember that this is your first time at the beach. So, you walk down to the sea and you have a paddle. The water washes over your toes, laps up to your ankles, maybe you even wade out until you're knee-deep.

As you get used to being in the sea, your confidence increases. You walk a little deeper, with the water reaching your waist, up to your elbows and eventually your chest. Then, you're swimming. At this point, some people get bitten by the bug for the ocean. They decide they love being in the sea. Those people might buy a mask, snorkel and fins and go snorkelling. They start to see the fish underwater, all the wildlife that lives on the sand. It's exciting, but it's a bit more risky than paddling or swimming.

Then there are people who love what they see from the surface so much that they decide to go scuba diving. They have an air cylinder on their back and all the gear that allows them to go deeper. They have a totally different view, but there's more pressure and there's more risk than staying at the surface.

Finally, you have the people who go all out. They go deeper and deeper, wearing all kinds of technical equipment and specialist suits to take them to the bottom of the ocean.

What does going to the beach and scuba diving have to do with financial simplicity? I'm going to show you how this analogy applies to investing.

At the beach

If you're sitting on the beach just watching the ocean, you've got all of your money in the bank. You'll be moving your money from bank to bank to try and get a slightly higher rate of interest. That's a lot like regularly applying suntan lotion to prevent sunburn.

The problem is that if you sit in the sun for too long, you're going to get sunburn even if you apply lotion. Similarly, you'll lose out if you leave your money in the bank for too long. The interest rates the bank offers will never beat inflation, so over the long term you will avoid some of that 'burn' by moving your money around from bank to bank, but you won't be able to avoid all of it.

Getting into the sea

When you decide that you want to beat inflation, you need to dip your toe into the ocean of investment. To do that, you need to enter the equity market. Let's say that initially you decide to invest 100,000 (the currency doesn't matter), we would put 20% of your funds into the equity market. We'll put the other 80% of your money that you're prepared to invest into safer investments like government and corporate bonds. It's important to stress that these aren't entirely safe, but they are safer than equity markets.

This is like going paddling. A small percentage of the money you're willing to invest is in stocks and shares, which represents a small risk. Once you've taken that step, you leave that 20% for a period of time. As you get more confident, you might increase the amount you've got in equity markets to 40%. That's the equivalent of going for a swim.

When you're feeling really comfortable there, you might increase that further to 60% of your money being invested in equity markets. Now you're snorkelling. As soon as you go to 80% or more of your money in the likes of stocks and shares, you're entering scuba diving territory. It's quite volatile and it's risky.

No diving allowed

I work through a risk tolerance questionnaire with every client to ascertain their attitude to risk. Depending on their circumstances, they might be able to go straight to snorkelling, with 60% of their funds invested in stocks and shares. Or maybe they're nervous having spent so long sitting on the beach, so we start by going for a paddle and just investing 20%.

But I have a rule in my company that there's no diving allowed. We're not going to expose our clients and their money to that level of risk and, if they've been sitting on the beach trying to build up the courage to jump in, we'll take it slowly rather than diving in at the deep end. Even if we complete the risk tolerance questionnaire and they come back as a balanced investor, we'll start them off from the position of a cautious or defensive investor, just to build up their confidence.

There's also no pressure to reach the level of scuba diving. I will check in with them to find out whether they want to go from paddling to swimming. But if all they ever need to do to achieve all of their goals is to go swimming, then that's what we'll do. There's no need for them to go snorkelling or scuba diving and expose themselves to that level of risk if they don't need to.

Remember the lifeguard

What I want all my clients to remember is that, firstly, they don't need to rush into the sea and, secondly, that they don't need to go into the sea alone. I'm like their lifeguard on the beach, watching over them as they start to paddle. I'll even get wet and go for a swim with them if that's what they need in order to feel confident taking the next step.

It's really important to have a lifeguard watching over you in case you get a bit out of your depth and start struggling, or if you don't understand how the tides work and are a little unsure of how things will work out. I'm the lifeguard, who's there to hold out a helping hand and make sure they're ok. I'm also there to rescue them in case they become a bit overconfident and get swept out to sea.

That's my role as a financial planner: to watch over my clients' investments, to make sure they're taking sensible risks and to keep them safe if they push things a little too far.

How does this keep things financially simple?

If you've spent all of your time chasing interest rates by moving money from bank to bank to bank, you'll have an account here, an account there, and before you realise it you could have five, ten, fifteen or even more accounts where you're saving your money. My personal client record is 27, yes 27 different accounts...... that client now has a maximum of five.

You can tell yourself that you don't want to put all of your money in one place because you want to spread the risk and make sure it's distributed across the marketplace, but with all of the protection available from the Financial Services Compensation Scheme (in the UK your savings are protected from your bank going under, up to certain limits), you really don't need to worry about not having enough cash available to you if a bank goes under. Rather than having your money spread across 20+ accounts, you can simplify it so that you know exactly what you have and where it is.

All you need are a couple of bank accounts, one for your salary and one to pay all your bills, premium bonds, a general investment account, an ISA account and a pension pot. That's pretty much it for most people!

When to start investing

Whether you're just building up your savings or you're rebuilding after a financial disaster, there are some simple steps you should take to put yourself in the position for investing.

Firstly, you should make sure you're in the position where you have three months' worth of money to cover whatever your monthly bills are, as well as your food. Don't forget about your food – it's all well and good covering all of your bills, but if you can't afford to eat you'll be dead! Let's take an average couple in the UK who may earn circa £40,000–£60,000 per annum. Having this three months' worth of money set aside means that if you lose your job or your income dries up, you have a bit of cash to tide you over and you don't need to grab for the first thing that comes along.

Once you've saved that figure of three months' worth of money, look to double it. That will give you six months' worth of money, which for most people will be between £10,000 and £15,000. That can sit in your bank or premium bonds and act as your emergency fund. When you have this amount of money available, you can start to think about investing. But the vast majority of people don't have anywhere near that amount of money in their bank or building society as an emergency fund.

If you don't have that much saved up in your account, but are thinking about investing, my advice to you is to stay on the beach a little bit longer to build up your confidence and build up that reserve fund.

Remember that sometimes you can achieve your goals without taking anywhere near the amount of risk that you think you need to take. Very often, it's a case of being consistent. In fact, I'd say that saving consistently over a longer period will get you a better return than being very, very risky.

Don't rush into deep sea diving. Spend time paddling, learn to swim and become really proficient at it before you dive into the deep end.

Chapter 2: The 100k Club

Setting your income goal

The 100k Club is a concept based around setting income goals. Earning £100k was the first income goal I set myself. This was also the qualification to sign up for the Strategic Coach® Program, although I had been to many taster sessions (so many that Paulette Sopoci, a presenter at many of the sessions I attended, thought I must be on the Program).

I started thinking seriously about setting goals around my income when I qualified for the Million Dollar Round Table (MDRT). Founded in 1927, MDRT, The Premier Association of Financial Professionals®, is a global, independent association of more than 72,000 of the world's leading life insurance and financial services professionals from more than 500 companies in 70 nations and territories.

The income qualification for MDRT was around £55,000 to £60,000, so when I reached it I was in the top 5% of financial advisers globally.

At this time, I read a book by Jack Canfield. In it, he talked about how he wrote a cheque for $1 million and stuck it to the ceiling above his bed, so that it was the last thing he saw before he went to sleep and the first thing he saw when he woke up. Personally, the last thing I want to see before I go to sleep is my wife, but whatever works for you!

This was the time when I first started setting myself goals, and the first goal I wrote down was for my business to make £100k. You might think that I could have aimed higher, because although £100k is a lot of money, in the world of business this is still quite a modest figure. So yes, I could have set a loftier goal. But when you start goal setting it's important that you don't make your goals too big, or they can feel overwhelming and unachievable. Be realistic; if you're only earning £20,000 but set your sights on earning £1 million within a couple of years, your brain goes, 'Nope, not going to happen' and then (guess what?) nothing happens.

You need to be a bit modest with your expectations, but remember that when you achieve a goal, you can then set a bigger one because you've got more confidence.

Why £100k?

The £100,000 figure just made sense to me. This was also the qualification to sign up for the Strategic Coach® Program, which I was keen to join having been to many of their taster sessions. I was already earning over £50,000 in my business, so it wasn't too much of a stretch to see it increasing to that £100k. As I got closer to that £100k figure, and then when my turnover surpassed it, everything made sense. It was time to set a new goal.

I decided to stick with the £100k figure because I was familiar with it, but this time I was aiming for £100,000 in net profit, not just turnover. With all the expenses I have, that meant turnover in my business needed to be closer to £130,000, so that the figure I put on my annual tax return could be £100,000 in net profit.

For me, having that £100k as a goal has worked for a multitude of progressions. It's one that you can concentrate on without making it too hard for the reticular cortex in your brain, which is vital for goal setting. In case you're not familiar with the reticular cortex, this is the part of your brain that filters out all the external stimuli and allows you to focus. You just have to tell it what you want. In this case, I told it I wanted £100k, first in turnover and then net profit.

Of course, you can't stick with £100k forever. Once I reached £100k in net profit, I decided it was time for a bigger goal. This time, I decided I wanted £200,000 in turnover, and so the process started again. Reaching this income goal also ticked another goal off my list, which was to qualify for Court of the Table of the MDRT, putting me in the top 2%(ish) of financial advisers globally. I achieved this based on my production for the year ending 2014, remembering that just three years earlier I was on the edge of bankruptcy.

But as I was getting close to that £200,000 figure for my turnover, I decided I should increase it to £250,000. I first wrote that as a goal in late 2013. When my wife Bonnie did my accounts for the year ending March 2019, lo and behold, my turnover was a little over £250,000 (well, £250,266 to be exact). Ok, it took me a while to move from under £200,000 to just over £250,000, but sometimes I am a slow learner, and I get distracted along the way.

It was crazy to see that I was less than £1,000 over that goal figure. At this point, I decided I should change my goal again to be something more sensible. In March 2018, I had a feeling that we were getting close to the £250,000 figure, so I increased my goal to £500,000. As you saw earlier, my premonition was right; we were going to hit £250,000 and in fact had exceeded it by a very small margin. It's important to be aware of what is going on, and adjust your goals accordingly. At the time of writing in the first quarter of 2020, I can say that as of 31 December 2019, I've reached that goal. Naturally, I can't go into the specific reasons behind how more than £500,000 has legally made its way into my bank account, but it's there, with a similar amount received in 2020. The reticular cortex was working for me all along as I've reached another of my income goals, and all the hard work has paid off.

Why setting income goals is important

Setting goals of any kind is important. They help keep you on track, even when you write them down, put them in a drawer and don't look at them for several years. There's a reason why goal setting works. Your subconscious brain can't tell the difference between the truth and the subliminal message. It just takes what you're feeding it as gospel.

When it comes to your income, you need to focus. Otherwise, especially when you're doing ok, you find that you're meandering through life. When you meander, you spend too much money and that means things will never improve for you.

I was in the same situation until I started my 100k Club. I was making money in the business, I was doing ok, but then a tax bill would come along and all the money would get spent on that. Setting an income goal is smart. It makes sense to have a goal to earn a certain amount of income, because then not only can you make sure you've got enough to pay your taxes, but more importantly that you've got enough to live your life the way you really want to live it.

How to start your own 100k Club

Thinking about goals is one thing, but writing them down creates a proper connection in your brain, which is why written goals are more effective than just thoughts.

Think about the last time you left the house to go shopping, and as you were walking out of the door your partner said, 'Can you get two loaves of bread and a pint of milk?' You say, 'Yes.' But although it goes in, it doesn't stick. As soon as you get to the supermarket, you find yourself wandering around the aisles thinking, 'What was I supposed to buy?' This is why I always write a list in my phone, because firstly it makes a proper connection, so I'm more likely to remember it, and secondly it acts as a fail-safe in case I forget.

But it's the same with your goals. Writing them down is important because it creates that connection within your brain and this means you're more likely to achieve them. That's the first step to creating your own 100k Club, writing down your income goals (and your other goals, but we'll come to those later).

Because your brain accepts what you're telling it, you need to write your goals in the present tense. For example, 'I drive', 'I earn', 'I am happily married', and so on. It's about placing your focus in the right place.

Take me as an example. If you looked at my desk, which is invariably covered in dozens of post-it notes, paperwork and goodness knows what else, you would probably wonder how I get anything done, let alone run a business turning over £250,000 with just two part-time members of staff.

There are always dozens of small jobs that are vying for your attention, but which of those is going to get you closer to your goals, whether that's in terms of your income or something else you're aiming for? By writing out your goals, you're showing your brain where to focus and what distractions to cut out.

One of the reasons why I'm able to cut out a lot of those distractions is because my two part-time members of staff are great at digging into the detail and following through on jobs. They're the opposite of me in that respect. I take initiative, I start things, but I'm not good at following through and completing those things. In my team, we all play to our strengths. I can come up with new ideas and get projects started, and my team are great at taking those ideas and seeing them through to completion.

Because they take those distractions away from me, I'm able to focus on the areas that are important not only for my income goals, but for my other goals as well.

As I mentioned earlier in the chapter, when you're setting goals, especially around your income, you need to be realistic. Goals have to be **SMART** (I'll talk more about this in the next chapter).

When you're working in financial services, the sky is almost the limit for your income. There will be thousands and thousands of people within a three-mile radius of where you live and work who need your help. But what you have to remember is that it will take time and practice to get there. We all have to start somewhere, and I would say that a good place to start with your income goal is quite a bit above making ends meet.

Start at the beginning so that you know what that figure is. Know what it's going to take for you to be earning to make ends meet. And if that's what you have to do right now, focus on that. Keep it simple and change your goals as you and your business grow.

This isn't so much about the £100k, but about the goal to get there. You have to work out whatever that figure needs to be and join whatever club works for you.

Why this isn't a SMART goal

We all know that our goals need to be smart, but knowing that is different to knowing what defines a smart goal. There can be slight variation in how you define a smart goal, but I believe there are five key elements to a SMART goal.

A goal needs to be:

- **S**pecific
- **M**easurable
- **A**chievable
- **R**ealistic
- **T**rackable

Then it's SMART.

The title of this chapter is 'Happy Wife, Happy Life', but is that a SMART goal? I would argue it's not. Why?

Is it specific...? No, because it doesn't define happiness.

Is it measurable...? No, because it relates to someone else's emotional state.

Is it achievable...? No, because no one can be happy all the time.

Is it realistic...? No, again because no one can be happy all the time.

Is it trackable...? No, because your state of happiness fluctuates.

I'm not saying you should give up on trying to make your wife happy, far from it. But what I am saying is that, in terms of goal setting, this isn't a smart goal to have. It's not something you can achieve.

When you get a goal that becomes impossible and doesn't fit the SMART criteria, you have to change it. I realised this and changed my goal from 'having a happy wife' to 'having a happier wife'. This goal is always a work in progress, but it's also something you can always work towards.

My story with my wife isn't uncommon. Like a lot of people in my position, self-employed, running my own business from home, I worked with my wife Bonnie. While it's great to have a supportive partner, working together isn't always a smart idea.

Bonnie and I worked together for eight years (from 2006 to 2014) before we acknowledged it wasn't a smart idea. Remember that Michelle Hoskin (who wrote the foreword for my book) told you that she met me in June 2011 and told me that I needed to 'sack Bonnie'? Well, it took me three years to sack Bonnie.

During the first two weeks that Bonnie worked for me, she cried multiple times during her training. We'd argue, I'd lose my patience. I'm the first to admit that my training style isn't the best in the world, but after those two weeks she said something that really hit home.

Bonnie said, 'I know that you're considerably more patient with your clients than you are with me.' And she was right, but to me that felt wrong. We should all be as calm, patient, gentle and kind with our significant others as we are with the rest of the world. But more often than not, we aren't.

For those eight years, Bonnie helped the business a lot. She got stuck in and did a lot of the admin work, but she didn't enjoy it. We reached a point where I realised she needed to do something else, so I told her that I thought she needed to find something that she wanted to do, rather than helping me because she thought she should.

Bonnie's initial concern was that she'd have to find a part-time job to pay the income of the person who came in and took her admin job. But what I realised was that, if I had someone working for me, as my employee, I could tell them exactly what I wanted them to do. There wouldn't be any arguments, I would be kinder and together we'd get more work done and probably generate more business.

Having a part-time employee would allow me to concentrate on the things I needed to do, knowing that I had a support person doing the jobs that I wanted them to do. Having the opportunity to concentrate in this way did, indeed, bring in more business and that's how we made up the money we needed to pay for that person. Bonnie has continued to do the books, which she enjoys, but now she doesn't do any of the admin tasks, which she hated.

Instead, she has developed her interest as an interior house stylist, which she loves. It also helps me achieve one of my goals which is to have an immaculately presented house, as Bonnie is constantly working on our home, but honestly being able to step away from the admin and focus on what she enjoys has made her happier. I've achieved my goal of having a happier wife. Two for the price of one, not bad!

When you're setting goals, you have to keep asking yourself if they're SMART. Are they specific? Are they measurable? Are they achievable? Are they realistic? Are they trackable? If the answer to any of those questions is 'no', you have to change the goal so that you come up with five 'yeses'.

Think back to the last chapter and setting your income goal. If you say that you want to have £1 million in turnover but you only have 15 clients, that's not realistic and that makes it demotivating. Whereas, if you set your goal for £100,000 in turnover, that's specific, it's certainly measurable, and for anyone working in financial services it's achievable and therefore realistic. You can track your progress towards it and see when you've reached it. It's a SMART goal.

These conditions don't just apply to financial goals. They apply to goals in all areas of your life. You might want to lose weight, drive a specific car (or in my case it's a motorcycle – first it was a Harley Davidson 1200 custom and then my Harley Davidson Fatboy Special; I got the 1200 custom in 2006/7 but had to sell it in 2012, at which point I started craving the Fatboy), have a certain amount of time off, and so on. Whatever goals you have, if you make them SMART you can achieve them.

Set goals early

I strongly advise you to start setting goals as early as you can in your business life. At the time of writing this, I'm 57 years old. At this stage of my career, do I want to be building an organisation where there are five financial advisers, 20 admin staff and a monthly advertising budget of £20,000 to generate leads? The answer is probably not.

If you're 30 or 35 and you're getting started in the industry, there's no reason why you can't build a massive organisation, but you need to understand what that entails.

I think that to have a self-funding business in the financial services industry, you need a business that's turning over at least £1.5 million a year. That will allow you to employ a business manager, three or four financial advisers and admin staff, as well as have the budget for marketing, and still make money for yourself at the end of it.

To achieve this, you've got to set your goals early and set your processes up to enable the business to grow. You need to decide that this is the kind of business you want, rather than a lifestyle business where you, as an individual, are still dealing with people and customers.

Remember that your first goal when you're starting out should always be to make ends meet, plus your tax on top. Don't forget about the tax! If you've only got to turn over £40,000 to make ends meet, but you have to give £7,500 to the taxman at the end of the year, then actually you need to bring in £50,000 to make ends meet.

Always remember the SMART acronym, and if a goal is impossible then you change it. We want to be working towards having a happier wife, rather than the impossible ideal of a happy wife.

Chapter 4: Leaving the Garden Shed Behind

Setting up your environment

Most of us accept that we need to have the right kind of environment in order to be productive at work. But when you're starting out it can be difficult to create the kind of professional environment you need to launch and grow your business. Financial advisers or many small businesses often start by working out of their own homes. While I've been there and done that, I'm going to explain why you need to make finding a dedicated office space a priority.

Starting out

When I started my business I was living in a smaller property than the one I have now. Many financial advisers find themselves in this position, where you're either working from the bedroom, the dining-room table or the kitchen. You've got your laptop and files everywhere and things can get a bit messy. If you're living with a partner, it can be especially difficult.

In the house that Bonnie and I shared at this time, there wasn't any space for a separate office, so we bought a shed for the garden. I'm doing it a disservice by calling it a shed, it was more like a garden room. It had electricity and an internet connection, so I worked from there for a year or so.

After about a year, my parents passed away and I received an inheritance, so we were able to move to a larger house with a fourth bedroom and a study downstairs. That made things easier, but it was still far from ideal. You can't really bring clients to your home. We also had dogs and, while I always thought they were an excellent judge of someone's character, again it's not ideal to be meeting clients in your home with your dogs racing about (although I do know one adviser who is making a success of working from home with llamas wandering around...).

It's hard to run a professional business from home in the financial services sector because you need to have those face-to-face meetings with clients.

When you want to employ someone to help you out, it also makes things difficult if you're working from home. When Bonnie and I moved, I had staff coming to our home to work for me. But it always felt a bit awkward to have my team members just wandering into the kitchen to make a coffee or tea, especially after Bonnie stopped working for me.

The other downside to working from your home is that it's difficult to switch off when you have reminders of your work right in front of you.

Finding your space

My first piece of advice, therefore, is to get yourself into a position where you're not working from home. One option is to explore serviced offices so that you can leave your garden shed or bedroom behind.

When you start looking for an office, think about both what you need it for now and what you'll need it for in the future. Don't forget that, even when you're just setting out, you'll still have bulky furniture like filing cabinets that take up space and can make a relatively small office feel cluttered and messy. It's worth investing in a slightly larger office if you can afford to, and certainly consider going paperless from the outset if you can!

Once you've got a separate office, it also makes it much easier to hire an administrator, and they are what I would consider the next best investment you can make for your business. Consider how you will fit another person (or people) into your office. It makes sense to invest in a slightly larger office than you need initially to enable you to grow.

You should also think carefully about how you set up your working environment. For example, we have one large office with a smaller office within it, which is my domain. It's ideal because it means I can close the door when I need some peace and quiet, and it gives me a private space to meet clients in. It also allows me to have some separation from my team. It's great to be available, but sometimes you need time to work without interruptions.

For me, setting up your environment is essential for helping you find a good work-life balance.

Working efficiently

When you have an office, it also allows you to work more efficiently. As a financial adviser who's working from home, you will spend a lot of time travelling between client meetings. You can't ask them to come to you, so you have to go to them, and that means a lot of wasted hours in the car each day.

Once you have an office, you can ask people to come to you. While that might mean you reduce your sphere of operations slightly, because some people won't be prepared to travel an hour or so to your office, it will allow you to be much more productive in your working day and make effective use of your time.

With modern technology and online video conferencing tools like Zoom, there's no reason why you can't keep your clients who are based further away and predominantly work with them using virtual systems.

Don't let your office hold you back

If you work from your home for too long, or your office is too small to allow you to grow your team, you'll be stunting the growth of your business. As a financial adviser, the most important factor for growing your business is having support from a team.

If you're working out of one room in your home, or even just a small one-room office, you'll quickly outgrow it. You need to think about where you'll store your files and make sure that you and your team aren't working on top of one another. Having a dedicated office that's large enough for your current needs and modest expansion gives you the opportunity to hire a team and grow more rapidly.

Having a proper office also supports your professionalism and how you come across to clients. But it's important not to fall into the trap of never feeling satisfied with your environment. It can be easy to think that you need somewhere bigger, or swankier, or nicer, or that you need new filing cabinets even though the ones you've got are perfectly serviceable.

You need to get the balance right between creating a funky environment that you're going to enjoy working in and that your clients will enjoy coming to, and one that clients are going to visit and start getting concerned about how much you might charge them. You want your office to reflect the fact that you're a high-quality organisation, but you need to get the balance right because it can be easy to get carried away.

Keeping your team happy

Your team are a vital part of your environment and you should want them to be happy when they're at work. Keeping your team happy doesn't have to cost a lot of money. Simple gestures can go a long way. I always make sure that my team have everything they're going to need for work. If they tell me they've run out of something, I'll make sure I order replacements to arrive the next day.

One of my team is quite short, so I bought her a little step to go under her chair and make sure she is comfortable at her desk. You should never hold back on small things like this. I've always found that if you're supportive of people's needs and give them what they ask for, within reason, they don't take the mick.

It doesn't cost you a lot of money as a business owner, but it keeps everyone happy and you can't put a price on that. It's important not to assume what will make people happy though. Ask your team what they need or want from their environment and do your best to provide it. Remember that everyone is different.

For example, I bring my team Lindt chocolate probably once every three weeks or so. It's just a small gesture but it creates an amazingly friendly atmosphere among the team. It's just a nice little perk and I make sure I don't always bring chocolate on the same day at the same point in the month so that it's always a nice surprise, rather than something people expect. It works both ways, too. One of my team bought me a bag of Revels the other day because they know how much I love those chocolates. It's a reciprocal thing that creates a happy working environment.

You'd be amazed by what you can achieve when you have a happy and friendly environment at work.

How you influence the environment

You have to remember that your disposition has as much of an impact on your environment as anything else and this is something you can control.

Sadly, there are some people who don't have the right disposition and they choose not to change it, whether that's because they're not happy with their lot, they're not happy with their environment or their expectations are just too high. You have to make sure that you are happy and friendly when you're around your team. Alternatively, you could spend your time replacing staff every couple of months. However, due to the time and the expense that goes with that, it's not a good alternative at all.

Likewise, you want to make sure that your environment gives you a positive feeling. For example, I find that I feel drained and lose motivation when my office is a mess and there are files and other bits and pieces everywhere. In fact, this happened not so long ago. On the Friday, my team told me not to worry and, sure enough, when I came in on Monday morning they'd tidied everything up and I instantly felt more positive.

It's important to remember that being in a cramped and messy environment will affect your mood, probably make you grumpy and add to not only your stress but also your team's stress.

Just be nice

My golden rule is to be nice to everybody, whether that's your clients, your team, your suppliers, your lenders or your providers. The world goes round much better and you get things done so much more quickly when you're nice.

If I need help with something, I often start my conversations with the phrase, 'Look, I'm in a little bit of a pickle and I really need some help.' And if they're a reasonable human being, they'll want to help you.

By contrast, if you pick up the phone and start screaming and shouting, or effing and jeffing, at the person on the other end, they'll say everything you want to hear just to get you off the phone. But I guarantee if your file is in a pile of 20 others, it won't be getting anywhere near the top soon.

I'll close this chapter with a story about why it pays to be nice.

I was in India and I lost my passport. The frustrating thing was that it fell out of my pocket on the plane and I knew exactly where it would be, only, of course, I couldn't go and retrieve it. That meant I had to go to the consulate in New Delhi to get a new passport. Luckily, the guy I was with was a police officer, so he could sign my passport photo. That meant I was able to get a new passport within 24 hours.

But that wasn't the only thing I needed in order to continue my travels. I also needed to apply for a new exit visa. I was due to leave two days later, but I wouldn't be able to get my flight without that visa. I had to miss a trip to the Taj Mahal to stay in New Delhi and sort all of this out.

The visa office was quite busy and there was a girl there who wanted to catch a flight that night. She also needed an exit visa and she kept pleading, not very nicely, almost indignantly, with the customs officer to deal with her application next. She went on and on, telling him that he had to deal with her application, and he kept telling her that he didn't and would get to it in time.

At one point, he left his desk and I watched her reach behind and move her application higher up the pile on his desk. Of course, when he came back he noticed and he made a specific point of moving her application back down the table. All I kept thinking was, just be nice. Maybe if she had been nice he would have dealt with her application more quickly, and she could have made her flight. I managed to get on mine. Think about it: a replacement passport and an exit visa in New Delhi in less than three days, just be nice. I do need to go back to India, as I still haven't seen the Taj Mahal.

Chapter 5: When There's Too Much Month at the End of the Money

Budgeting and clearing debts

I'd like to start by telling you how I learned the hard way about the importance of budgeting and clearing debt.

It was 2007 and I'd just received my inheritance after my parents passed away. Bonnie and I bought our new, bigger house and moved in, in August of that year. The business was doing well. I was arranging 15 to 20 mortgages a month, as well as all of the life insurance that goes with them. We had a big mortgage on the house, but that wasn't a problem. I bought myself a decent Mercedes, which was one of my goals, a coupe, using a bit of finance. Everything was great. Until...

The global financial crisis hit. It was as though the tap had been turned off. I went from arranging 15 to 20 mortgages a month for the majority of 2007 to probably doing a maximum of 25 mortgages for the whole of 2008. Our lives suddenly became very difficult. We had lodgers to help earn a bit of extra money. We rented out our driveway.

It became trickier and trickier to pay the mortgage and cover all of our bills and other bits and pieces. Before too long we'd racked up a six-figure debt. We were constantly juggling things around to try and make ends meet. By 2010, I realised we needed some help and we had to rearrange our finances to give us a more affordable monthly payment.

In spite of all of this, I still think we were lucky. We had support from our business network, which allowed us to continue working in financial services. I don't know what I'd have done if I hadn't been able to carry on in the industry. But this was an incredibly difficult time. We had no spare money whatsoever. As you can imagine, Bonnie wasn't happy. But I still needed to focus on the business.

Because we weren't able to borrow any money, we had to develop the business on a shoestring budget. I poured all of my energy into making sure that all of my clients were looked after and that we were providing as good a standard of advice as we possibly could.

Learning to avoid temptation

One of the tricky things when you're in this situation is that you can be attracted to areas that you don't fully understand because you want to make some extra money. That was exactly the trap I fell into around this time.

The service I started offering, that I didn't know enough about, was stamp duty mitigation. This is a specialist tax scheme to circumvent the normal tax due on a house purchase. At the time, the idea was that you could purchase a house in a creative way to avoid having to pay stamp duty, and the organisation who set up the purchase would instead receive half of the stamp duty cost as a fee.

It's not directly financial services, but it's related. However, it wasn't my area of expertise. To cut a long story short, a couple of the purchases I set up failed and I lost my clients a lot of money. The firm doing the planning went into administration, so we were unable to refund the fees charged, and the taxman came calling for the full stamp duty. These were clients I'd describe as influential and potentially highly profitable who blamed me for a substantial loss and, as a result, stopped using my services. That was a big lesson for me to not get involved in things I don't fully understand that are outside my area of expertise.

I would advise that when you're under pressure financially, you take extra care about what you let your mind think about and what you get involved with. It's easy to be tempted by the promise of extra money now, but if, like me, things don't work out as you planned it can cost you more in the long term than you gain in the short term.

Budgeting from the start

One of the best pieces of advice I can give you is to think very carefully about your budget when you start your business. Look very carefully at how much you need to earn to make ends meet. You need to know what your bills are to live, as well as what your bills are for running your business. That includes everything from the cost of your office, to things like advertising because, at the beginning, you're going to need to spend quite a bit on advertising and marketing to get the word out there. The most important thing is to make sure that you have a budget for all of these expenses.

You also have to make sure that you're sensible about how you spend your money once you start earning. You might have a solid month of income, way more than you need, but don't rush to spend all the money you're making above your outgoings. My advice would be to put this extra money in reserve.

Let's take a look at an example budget to see how much money you'll need to be making to cover all of your expenses.

Imagine that all of your personal bills - that's the mortgage, energy, broadband, phone, food and so on - come in at £3,000 a month. Then you need to allow another £1,000 a month for running the business, covering your fees for transacting and so on. On top of that, you need to allow money for tax, because the taxman will want to take his slice regularly too.

Tax is something that a lot of people forget about. If you've earned £3,000 a month that's £36,000 in annual profit, which means, to all intents and purposes, you've got another £8,000–£10,000 in tax to allow for. It's not something you want to forget in your calculations or you're in for a nasty surprise! I had far too many of those in my early years...

You also need to know how much you are going to charge for your services. I have had a number of conversations and seen examples where the session/ service rate charged to make ends meet meant that the number of clients needed was more than one could realistically see in a week/month. Say you need to earn £3,000pm, your session is £50.00, which means you need to do 60 sessions per month, which is only 15 per week, or three per day. That doesn't sound a lot, but when you do some market research you find that a busy established business is doing five per day, and sometimes less. You are starting from scratch and you need to dive in at 60% capacity of an established business from day one. You are also travelling to see your clients, so now you need a decent car and you need to cover the cost of fuel. Before you know it, to net £3,000 you have to do more business each month than the established business. Pay very careful attention to your figures and your targets, make them SMART.

The difference between being a salesperson and running a business

What you have to remember when you set up your own business is that it's not the same as being a salesperson. Of course, you need to sell, but there's so much more to it than that. This is a mistake that a lot of people who've spent their lives working at firms make.

When you're working for a firm, you might be an amazing salesperson, taking

£10,000 of sales a month. But you have to appreciate all the support you're getting there that allows you to make those sales, and that support doesn't cost you a penny while you're an employee. I'm talking about admin support, people answering the phones, marketing support and so on.

When you go out on your own, you've got to do all of that yourself. All of a sudden, you can't spend your whole day selling because you have to make time to do all the admin, the accounts, the marketing, answer the phones. You'll find that 60–70% of your time isn't spent on sales any more; it's spent on all those other tasks that you took for granted as being done by other people when you worked for a firm.

This then means that when you do meet with clients, you're under pressure to sell. Trust me when I tell you that when you're under pressure to make a sale, a client knows it. You can be the best actor in the world, but I guarantee they'll be able to tell when you're desperate to make a sale.

My advice when you're starting out is to set your expectations at a reasonable level. Make sure that you account for everything, both in terms of your budget and what you'll need to spend your time doing.

How to market your business on a shoestring

As I mentioned earlier, following the financial crash we were forced to run our business on a shoestring. We didn't have the money to send our clients swanky brochures, but there are lots of small and cheap – if not free – things you can do to market your business.

We focused on keeping in touch with our existing clients on a regular basis in the most affordable way possible: email. I wanted to make sure that they had everything they could possibly need and that they got the best service possible, because that meant I was more likely to get referrals. These are a big factor in being successful in your business.

Even if you're operating on a budget, don't use that as an excuse to not have certain things. In the last chapter I talked about leaving the garden shed behind and setting up the right environment. This is absolutely worth doing even when you don't have a lot of spare money available.

If you look around, you can find affordable serviced offices where you can operate from. How affordable is going to depend on where you're based, but there are opportunities in most places; and by setting up in an office space rather than continuing to work from your shed, you'll find new clients and make new, often bigger, deals.

Before I moved out of my house into a serviced office, I used to go to the gym quite regularly, and on my way there, I'd pass a building that had a sign up for serviced offices. One day, Bonnie mentioned how nice it was on a Friday because I'd always be out and about that day, and my staff didn't work on Fridays. She said it was great to have the house to herself, and that was the not-so-subliminal trigger for me to look for a dedicated office space.

Of course, I thought of the building I passed every day, so I took a space in this serviced office. For a start, it was great at helping me stick to a working regime. But there was another benefit that I hadn't initially considered – I started meeting new people.

When you start working in a block of serviced offices, you'll be in there with all kinds of other people. You're quite likely to be the only financial adviser, so there's always a possibility that you'll pick up new business. Going back to the point I made in the last chapter about the importance of being nice, this applies when you're sharing a building with other businesses too.

A smile and a hello as you're walking down the corridor can go a long way. One of the simple things that we did was to put a branded notepad in everyone's pigeonhole at Christmas. It was our way of saying Merry Christmas and just letting everyone know that we were there. I also gave some to the maintenance office.

The nice thing is that a short while later one of the guys on the maintenance team came up to me to thank me for the notepad and tell me that it had been really useful. It also meant I got first options on a bigger office when it became available.

Now, this little gesture didn't cost us more than about £200 for around 150 notepads. It didn't take a lot of effort on our part either, but it did get us noticed and help me to start building relationships with the other people in the office building.

Don't forget about your personal life

I'll close this chapter by summarising the most important things to remember when it comes to budgeting and taking care of your money.

One of the keys is keeping an eye on your numbers and making sure that you don't forget people like the taxman when you're calculating your budget. Make sure you know how much it will cost you to exist each month. Once you know that, you can work out what you need to do month by month, business wise, to satisfy that need.

But while you're looking at your business costs and how much you need to make, don't take your eyes off your personal life. In fact, if you have a wife and you have a goal that you don't want her to have to work, account for this when you're calculating your budget.

I can tell you from experience that it's incredibly stressful for your relationship when you have too much month at the end of the money. When Bonnie and I were in this position and working together it caused a lot of stress. And stress is a killer. It doesn't only kill you in the literal sense, but it also kills your appetite for life and your 'get up and go'. You need to make time to talk about money and budget as a couple.

Whenever I sit down with a couple, I tell them to set up a joint account for their bills but to make sure they each keep their own personal account so that they can do nice things for themselves and their partner without them necessarily knowing how much it costs. When I'm talking to a couple about this, I usually tell the guy to buy his partner a bunch of flowers every now and then and see how his world lights up. Normally she'll laugh and say that he never buys her flowers, but it's a nice thing to do just because; not because it's their birthday or your anniversary. Those small gestures make a difference.

The other thing to remember about having a joint account for bills is to make sure you transfer the amount for your share of the bills into it the day after payday (you've then paid all your bills on one day). However, once your money has gone into there each month, you can't think of it as your money any more. That money is spoken for and you shouldn't dip into it for any other reason. You have to protect it.

There are two other things that I advise people to save for by putting money aside each month: holidays (vacations) and Christmas. I'm always amazed by how many people seem to be surprised by Christmas. It always falls on 25 December and you know that it's going to come around every year, because it has for over 2000 years. Yet, every year, people get caught out. They put 'Christmas' on their credit card and then they have to find a way to pay it off afterwards. Whereas, if they just put £75 a month aside for 12 months, they'd have £900 to spend on Christmas, without having to go near a credit card.

My other piece of advice for you when it comes to the likes of Christmas is to spend your money on experiences that you can share with your loved ones rather than on material items. After all, there's only so much space in a house. The average garage doesn't have a car in it, but is instead somewhere that people store all manner of things they never or rarely use. Don't contribute to that problem, and try not to give in to the pressure to buy new material possessions you don't need.

The same principle applies with saving for holidays. Too many people put their holidays on their credit cards and then have the stress of paying them off afterwards, which often negates the good that a holiday does. If you put

£100 a month into your holiday fund, it means you can have a pot of money to spend on whatever kind of trip you want. The key is treating it like another bill and saving for it accordingly.

If you budget correctly and allow for all the costs of both your business and personal life, you will hopefully avoid running into the scenario of having too much month at the end of the money.

Sarah's Story

How does that sound?

In April 2018 I met Doug and this couldn't have come at a better time for me. I'm a mortgage and financial adviser in New Zealand, covering mortgages and risk insurance. I'd started my business in October 2015, adding risk insurance in 2017. I'm a single parent with teenagers, and still relatively new to financial services. By the time I met Doug my business had stopped. In February/March 2018, it was almost as though someone had just decided I wasn't going to have any more business.

However, although my business had slowed right down, I was still travelling to the Gold Coast in Australia for the first overseas conference being hosted by my network. I'd paid for the trip, so I decided I may as well go. Before I go to any conference I always like to see who the speakers will be and I'd noticed Doug in the line-up before I travelled. I even connected with him on LinkedIn before the conference and told him I was looking forward to hearing him talk. Of course, he replied and said he looked forward to seeing me there.

When Doug stood up on stage he told his amazing story. I'm a big believer in the idea that you can't get to the very top without being at the bottom, experiencing some ups and downs along the way and climbing back to the top. I don't believe you can go from the bottom to the top without some kind of dip in the middle. After Doug had told his story, I decided that I'd go over and introduce myself.

As well as meeting Doug, I also met his wife Bonnie and we even all went for coffee together. As if to demonstrate how small the world is, we even realised that Crawley, where Doug and Bonnie live, was where I'd lived with my now ex-husband many years ago. In fact, my father-in-law lived just 1.6 miles from Doug's office. That was the beginning of my friendship with Doug. When I look back I feel as though I was meant to meet him. I could have very easily not gone to the conference, because money was so tight in my business, and I could have just as easily not introduced myself to him after his talk.

But I went and I made the effort to meet him in person and those decisions have changed my life.

As I said, my business had stalled. At this point, I was making very little money. But I still had a mortgage to pay and, of course, I was supporting my children. I didn't have money coming in from elsewhere so I knew I needed to be successful with this. I couldn't take any more credit cards out and the ones I had were full. I actually had to borrow some money from friends and I was considering selling my car, just to get the $8,000–$10,000 out of that.

When I returned to New Zealand after that conference I was really struggling. I'm not someone who finds it easy to ask for help. In fact, I don't even like the phrase 'reaching out for help', but I stayed in touch with Doug and at some point I felt bold enough to ask him to help me. He was really lovely and told me that he'd be happy to chat to me every now and then.

This was around May/June 2018. Because there's always an 11, 12 or 13-hour time difference between the UK and New Zealand, Doug used to call me in the mornings when he was out walking his dogs, which meant it was evening for me. It was just perfect.

Doug and I used to check in once a week and we'd talk about my business. I used to tell him about specific clients and ask his advice. As soon as we started talking regularly, it was as though I had this little person on my shoulder called Doug talking to me all the time.

Reaching out was a really big thing for me to do, and I think at the stage that Doug and I started talking regularly, I was at the bottom of my heap. But what you realise is that if you're at the bottom of your heap, you're not going to see wealth come to you. It's about your mentality and focus, and making sure that you open up to the world so that good things can come to you.

Doug encouraged me to really think about how I was looking after my clients, how I was talking to them, what I'd do if they tried to reduce the amount of insurance they took out to a level below what they needed and so on. And this worked both ways; I knew that he was helping me a lot but I also helped him with some ideas for his business.

That was also a big confidence booster for me, to be able to give Doug some ideas and different words and phrases to use too. But that's the thing about connections like this – we're both different people with different personalities who use different words to speak to clients, and sometimes it can really help to have a different perspective.

Aiming for MDRT

Doug was determined to help me get to Million Dollar Round Table (MDRT). At this point, I hadn't been doing insurance for that long, but in your first year you can apply for MDRT as what's called an Aspirant, where you have to get 50% of the normal qualification you need. I remember that it went right to the wire that Christmas.

Doug was always encouraging me. He would ask me how much more I needed to get and then he'd make me work out how many months and weeks we had to go, and how many policies I'd need to sell in New Zealand to hit that figure. He got me to divide this down into weeks, rather than months, which made it feel more manageable. I'd always be thinking about which client was warm, which clients I could go back to. I qualified as an MDRT Aspirant that year and it was really exciting. There's a big MDRT annual conference and the MDRT members get their spaces first. Then there's a specific date in March when they open up spots to Aspirants.

Because of the time difference, I needed to be online at 2am in New Zealand to login and register for my space for the conference. That didn't go entirely smoothly but I eventually registered and then I was really excited that I'd get to see Doug again.

In June 2019, the MDRT conference was held in Miami. To get there, I had a 15-hour flight to Houston, then a stop before I could fly to Miami. On the morning that I was due to leave New Zealand, I didn't feel too good. After an hour and a half I realised it could be something serious, so I phoned an ambulance for myself. I was rushed to hospital where they discovered I had kidney stones. It was really painful and I was dosed up on morphine. I don't remember a great deal, except that every time I saw a doctor I'd ask if there was any chance I could fly the following day, because that would have enabled me to make it for the conference.

I remember one doctor leaning over me and saying, 'Sarah, you've had that much morphine that you're not going to be flying anywhere.' And so I had to miss the conference. The feelings that overwhelmed me can't be described. I was devastated at this moment.

But Doug didn't let me give up and he kept pushing me with goals throughout the year – he made sure it was always about the client. It went to the wire – 17 December 2019. I did my numbers and I'd qualified for MDRT as a full member. For some people, this might not seem like such a big thing, but

I've only been working in insurance for just over two years and to make the numbers you need to qualify for MDRT is pretty amazing. But, of course, due to the situation and travel restrictions with COVID-19, I won't be able to make the MDRT conference in 2020 either. However, I've already set new goals for MDRT 2021.

Why it's good to talk

One of the things I've realised is that when I talk to Doug he doesn't focus on my numbers, he focuses on my clients. It's interesting because that perspective is what makes all the difference and it's what Doug and I both have in common.

No matter what we do, we want the client to get whatever's in their best interest. That means we're not only asking the client about their finances – their numbers – but we want to know about them as people and their experiences. That means the advice you can give them is framed in a different way.

The pause

I talk very quickly, and it's one of the things that Doug has helped me to moderate. He'll often say something and then pause. He's been trying to teach me to pause more because this makes the client really think about what you're saying. It's one of the most important things I've learned from him.

Seeing my business grow

I started my business from home in 2015 and within a year I'd moved into an external office, which happened to be very smelly due to nearby restaurants. The lease came up and I moved into a tiny space, 6m x 2m in size and relatively cheap to rent. But it wasn't a great space as it was so small and not ideal for bringing clients into. Ever since I started my business, I've been very clear that I need my clients to come to me – either to my office or to have virtual meetings via Zoom. I decided this was my business model. But as I said, this space was just too small. I also realised that I needed an assistant but I didn't have space for one.

In June 2019, the business that was leasing the rest of the floor that my tiny office is on moved out. I saw an opportunity so I leased the whole floor. By August, I was able to hire my first full-time employee, Helena. I gave her the title Client Manager. I didn't want to just call her my assistant, because she's so much more than that. I made a very conscious decision to take someone on full-time and to pay them a good salary, because I wanted a good person.

When I look back now at where I was just one year earlier, April 2018, at rock bottom and reaching out for help from Doug, I'm amazed. My initial goal was to build my income back up and put myself back out there. I hadn't considered that in just 12 months I'd have acquired a much bigger office and my first full-time employee.

I spoke to Doug a lot before I hired anyone into my business. We discussed the type of person I needed and the type of personality. It's been a big learning curve for me because I'd always been a manager of people and now I'm a doer. But after four years in business, I suddenly had to learn to let someone else do the work. Luckily I don't have to micromanage Helena at all, but then that's why I hired her. One of the things you always hear is that you should hire an assistant when you're not quite ready for one, otherwise if you wait you'll be too busy and won't have the time to train them properly. So it was a leap of faith for me but one that has really paid off.

Riding the ups and downs

I started my business in October 2015, so at the time of writing that's almost five years ago. I've been on a crazy journey in that time and I can honestly say I don't think I'd be where I am now if it weren't for Doug and his advice and support.

When I started my business, it just seemed to be on an upward trajectory. The business was never quiet and it was all going well. But when it started to slow down I was really scared. I have a nice house, which I'd just finished renovating, and I was seriously worried I was going to lose everything. I didn't have anyone to turn to who could support me and my children financially, and asking Doug for help with my business was really hard.

What this period made me realise is that it's not enough to be outgoing and engaging, because you really need to know your stuff when you hit hard times. After speaking to Doug, I got the business rolling again and this period was actually really cool. I was able to pay back the friends I'd borrowed money from and clear my credit cards to get rid of that debt. Then it was as though I could breathe again, thank goodness.

After sorting out all my personal financial things, it was great to be able to focus on growing the business. It's been wonderful to see the transformation, especially in my office. It's really nice to be able to see where I started out, in my tiny 6m x 2m office, and compare it to where I am now: a 92sqm office that I've even renovated so that it's an enjoyable space to be in. I know without a shadow of a doubt that I couldn't have got my business back on track and achieved all of this without Doug's support.

He could tell that I was excited, that I knew my stuff and that I wanted to learn, and that's why we got on. I'm really proud of what I've achieved and that I'm able to show that women of any age can succeed in this industry. In

2019, I won three really big awards too. All of that has helped improve my credibility with clients, who can walk into my office and see those awards displayed on the wall.

Connecting, communicating and confidence

One of the reasons why I think I really hit it off with Doug and why we've become such good friends is that he understands how I do business. I'm not the type of person who's comfortable cold calling people. Most of my clients come from contacts, referrals and connecting with people. My business leads by mortgages first, and looking after the client as a whole, and then risk insurance fits perfectly.

I also find clients through my work as a marriage celebrant. I've been working as a celebrant since 2009, which feeds in perfectly with my work as a financial adviser. Couples remember me and when they need help arranging a mortgage to buy their first home, or sorting out life insurance, they come to me.

I build strong connections with them because I remember little details about their wedding day. For example, there's one couple whom I married and whom I've helped a few times with organising financial products. On their wedding day, the weather wasn't great so we had to move the ceremony indoors. I was standing outside with Mary, the bride, ready to walk in for the ceremony and she turned to me and said, 'Sarah, I've forgotten my veil.' I looked at her and just said, 'You look fabulous. He's in there. He wants to marry you. He won't care about the veil.' And she walked straight in, and it was the most wonderful wedding. I find remembering small details like that about my clients' lives helps me to build those lasting connections, which then leads to them working with me in this business (along with me parking my branded car in the car park of the wedding venue!).

Communication is key to this. You need to talk and you need to listen. Doug and I communicate a lot. We talk. Sometimes I'll send him an email. It's the same with clients. You need to have regular catch-ups with them, whether that's face to face, via Zoom or just through a quick email.

It's not just about making connections with your clients either. It's about making professional connections. These are other advisers who can help you learn and grow your business, just like Doug has helped me to grow my business. It's an important mindset shift to go from seeing everyone as a competitor to realising that we're all different and that therefore we'll appeal to different kinds of clients.

The other thing I've learned from Doug is to have confidence in myself. You have to have the confidence to tell people your story, to explain how you fell down but then climbed back up again.

How does that sound?

This phrase, 'How does that sound?' is one of the most important things that Doug has taught me. Here's how it works.

I recently had a Zoom meeting with a couple whose wedding I performed in 2019. I've already done their insurance and at the moment I'm organising a mortgage for them. Sally and Bob are a lovely couple, you can just see that they're very connected. At the start of the meeting I asked them what was going on in their world, how their jobs are and so on. Bob told me that he's recently had a pay rise, so I just said, 'That's great, if you email me after this call I'll see if you need to get any more insurance. How does that sound?'

We carried on chatting and ran through the other things we needed to talk about. I always like to finish any client meeting by simply summarising what we've discussed. So, in this instance, I said, 'We'll just refresh what the next steps are. The next steps are that you're going to email me about your pay increase and I'm going to then check about an increase in your income protection. I'll also email you about the mortgage and we'll get that sorted in the next couple of weeks. We'll just keep the connection going. How does that sound?'

That phrase, 'How does that sound?' is useful for the client and for me. Firstly, it makes me stop talking because I'm asking a question. I have to pause. It's also a question that the client can't just say 'yes' or 'no' to. That makes them think about their answer.

It's about communicating and keeping those lines of communication open between you and your clients.

What you can learn from me

'How does that sound?' is one of my top takeaways from Doug, but there are a number of other things that you can learn from my story.

I would certainly say that I should have asked for help earlier, although I'm glad that I reached out when I did. Don't be afraid to reach out because you could end up with a wonderful friend like I did.

I'd also urge you not to dismiss the element of chance. Life is all about chance meetings. There were many times when Doug and I could have missed making that connection. I might not have sent him a message and connected with him on LinkedIn before the conference. I could have gone to see a different speaker that day. Or I could have chosen not to say anything to him after his talk, even though I'd been moved by it. The lesson is don't let those opportunities to meet people and connect pass you by.

You also have to remember that times change. You can't rest on your laurels. You always need to be looking for different things that you can do in business and how you can change if your business starts to stagnate. If you're a business that stays static and doesn't move with the times, you're going to get left behind.

Sometimes that might mean you have to drag your clients along with you. I've been using Zoom for meetings for a while, but with the COVID-19 pandemic that technology has suddenly become essential. If you've got a client who is a bit of a technophobe, look at how you can make the transition easier for them. How can you make it as easy as possible for them to access and engage with the technology you're using?

You also need to make sure you're always learning. That might be by doing training, but also just by talking to other advisers. Look at how much I've learned from Doug in the time I've known him.

The difference is Doug: a lifetime of business learnings in two years

If I was to sum up my friendship with Doug so far, I'd describe it as a lifetime of business learnings in two years.

I've been in the deepest, darkest financial place of my life, and come out the other side. I could have been forced to sell my house, even though that was the last thing I wanted to do. I could have lost my business. When I met Doug, I was at a very low point. With his help, I've been able to climb back up again. This was so lucky for me, my family and my business. I'm in such a great space now.

These things are meant to test us, but I honestly don't think I'd have come so far if I hadn't had a friend like Doug sitting on my shoulder, giving me guidance when I needed it. He's a priceless friend with so much knowledge to share and, more than that, he's happy to share it with anyone who asks.

How does that sound?

Sarah Bloxham

Financial adviser

Let's Talk! Mortgages & Insurance

Auckland, New Zealand

Chapter 6: It's a Given

Turning up on time

Trust is like a china plate. If it's broken, you can fix it, but the cracks will always show. That was a saying I first heard at my first MDRT meeting back in 1995 and it's always stuck with me. It encapsulates exactly why you need to be trustworthy and why you need to care about your clients. But more than that, they need to know that you care about them and they need to know that what you're doing for them is ahead of your own personal interests.

Gaining trust is simple and I'd say that turning up on time is a good starting point. It's one of the fundamentals from Dan Sullivan of Strategic Coach® too: say 'please' and 'thank you', turn up on time and always do what you've promised to do.

The only time I didn't turn up…

I can honestly say that there's only ever been one time in my career when I didn't turn up to meet a client. I received a phone call at about 10:10am on a Monday morning from Bev, the lady I should have been meeting, asking if I was coming.

I'm based in Redhill and when I got her phone call I wasn't remotely ready to leave the house. Not to mention that she lived in Berkhamsted, which is a 45-minute journey at the best of times. It was my mistake. I'd written our meeting in my day book, but I hadn't put it in my diary so I'd forgotten.

Now, I explained and managed to arrange another meeting with her, which was good, and she's given me plenty of business over the years. The point of this story is that you can make mistakes, and we all do, but you have to make sure that you do a little bit extra to overcome them. Bev holds the record for the most accounts at the beginning of our relationship: 27, I still cannot believe it!! Remember when I talked about financial simplicity in Chapter 1? There is just no need to hold that many accounts and I'm happy to report that Bev has no more than five accounts now.

The importance of being early

Aside from this meeting, I've always turned up and I'm always early. Turning up on time might be the subtitle of this chapter, but really it should be 'turning up early'. I would say that you should always aim to be at least ten minutes early for every meeting you're going to.

At one stage, I found myself in the situation where I was arriving for all of my meetings about half an hour early, because my assistant was significantly overestimating how long it would take me to get anywhere. I was getting reminders to leave for meetings earlier than I needed to, and I'd just go. I often found myself arriving somewhere at least 15 minutes early, sitting there twiddling my thumbs.

But what I realised was that those 15 minutes could be invaluable. During that time, I could visualise how the meeting would play out. I could consider the responses I might get from my client and any possible objections. It gave me time to think about how I could handle those and get the right outcome from the meeting. It meant I was calm and relaxed by the time I went in.

Contrast that to how you'd feel if you suddenly found out you had to leave the office for a meeting in 45 minutes and that it's a 45-minute drive away. You're rushing out of the door, grabbing files and paperwork as you go. Just as you get to the car, you realise you've left one of the files you needed in the office, so you run back in, get it and run back to the car.

Once you're in the car, you've got to put the address you're going to into your sat nav. While you're doing this time is ticking away, it takes three, four, five, six minutes before you're on your way. Now, all of a sudden, you're behind schedule for that 45-minute journey. You're shouting and screaming at all the other road users who, while they're driving perfectly normally, are holding you up. You get angry. You curse every red traffic light. Then you have to ring the client to tell them you're running ten minutes late.

What kind of mindset will you be in when you arrive for that meeting? You'll be flustered, your heart rate will be elevated, you won't be thinking clearly and you're much more likely to rush through what you have to say.

By turning up ahead of time, you're setting yourself up to be in control. You'll find that the deals you do are much bigger and that everything goes much more smoothly if you're even five minutes early for a meeting. In that time your heart rate can slow down, you can let your blood pressure drop and you'll feel more confident in the situation.

It's all about going into your meetings in the right mindset. You'll find that adding extra time to your schedule to allow you to turn up early will pay you back in dividends. You'll close bigger sales and create lasting relationships with clients.

Showing respect

Turning up early for meetings doesn't just allow you to feel more composed. It shows that you respect your client's time. If they've had to wait ten minutes for you that doesn't reflect well, especially if they're a busy person who doesn't have ten minutes to waste in their day. It puts you on the back foot and it comes back to breaking two of those fundamental rules from Dan Sullivan at Strategic Coach®: not only are you late, but you're not doing what you promised. You promised to turn up for a meeting at 10am and you haven't done that. It breaks trust.

The same rule of turning up early also applies to any online meetings you're hosting on platforms such as Zoom. You don't want to be the last person joining your meeting on Zoom when you're the host.

There's a flipside to this as well. Turning up early shows that you're respecting yourself. You're giving yourself permission and time to get into a relaxed state of mind. Rushing around all the time is also one of the quickest routes to a heart attack. You need to slow things down and stay in control. Respect your time and attitude as much as you respect your client's time.

Always be prepared

When you're rushing, you miss things and you forget things. If you race into a meeting late, you're not going to be calm and composed. You're probably not going to be logical and you'll almost certainly forget something important. As soon as something unexpected pops up, you'll lose all of your momentum. By the same token, you shouldn't turn up to meetings on time or early and try to run through everything off the cuff.

You need to be prepared. Create an agenda for every meeting you're going to, even if you decide not to share it with your client in advance – and there can be good reasons for not sharing agendas. But make sure you have one nonetheless.

As a financial adviser, I make sure I get my clients to fill in relevant paperwork well in advance of us having a meeting. I'll send them the risk questionnaire in advance. I'll get them to complete a medical form before I go to see them if we're looking at anything like life insurance or critical illness cover. If I'm going to see a client about arranging a mortgage I make sure they send me copies of their payslips and bank statements before our meeting.

There are several reasons why this is a good idea. Firstly, I want to make sure I have a full picture of my client, or as full as I can at this stage. I want to go to the meeting prepared with any paperwork I might need them to sign. You're shooting yourself in the foot if you go to a meeting without that critical piece of paper that will need their signature for you to make the sale.

Secondly, if you get someone to complete the risk tolerance questionnaire when you aren't there to lead or influence their answers, you'll get more honest answers from your client that will give you a truer picture of who they are. When it comes to risk tolerance questionnaires, they're also as dull as dishwater and you don't want to spend a whole meeting going through one. Trust me when I tell you that your job will be a lot more interesting if you get your clients to fill these forms in ahead of your meeting.

Thirdly, with the medical questionnaires, clients will feel more comfortable writing down their height/weight and so on if they're doing it on an anonymous form. When you speak to someone on the phone you can't possibly know that they're only five foot tall but weigh 19 stone. If you see that on a medical form, however, you already know that they're highly unlikely to ever get critical illness cover so you don't even bring that up as an option.

Doing all of this paperwork in advance allows you to be as prepared as possible. You can begin to assess someone's viability for life cover before you start sending them options. You can manage their expectations accordingly and you can make sure that they get the right cover for their circumstances and the best that you can find for them.

What you're doing by preparing for meetings in this way is ensuring that your client meetings are as productive as possible and that you spend time on what's appropriate. It's about making the best use of both your time and the client's time.

Learn to delegate

Accept that you need help to do your job properly and to the best of your ability. Delegating is essential, and delegating to the right person is just as important.

Ideally what you want to do is delegate all the tasks that you're weakest at to someone else. A person who not only enjoys but who is good at doing all the jobs you hate should be your first hire. When you're planning to hire an assistant, start by making a list of all the business tasks that you hate. They're probably going to be the ones you're no good at too. This list should form the basis of a job description.

Don't put off getting support for too long either. It's quite common in firms with multiple financial advisers to have a shortage of administrators. But if you don't have enough support with all of the admin tasks then there's no way you're going to be able to work at your greatest capability.

If you contrast the firms with, let's say, three financial advisers and two part-time administrators providing support, with the firms where one financial adviser has two or even three or four members of staff supporting them, you'll see that the latter are invariably more successful.

I personally think that no matter what you spend on staff you tend to get six or seven times their salary back from them in increased productivity. However, even if it is only twice as much but you have more free time, that's still a win in my book, so why wouldn't you want to get support with the admin as soon as possible?

Trying to do everything on your own also leads to situations where you turn up late for meetings. Picture the scene: you're just getting ready to leave the office when a phone call comes in, or an urgent email pops up in your inbox. Even if you don't answer the email or you take a quick phone message, this will pull your focus away from your meeting. You don't want to be running around like a mad thing all the time.

Hire an administrator and make sure that one of their jobs is to look at your emails. In an ideal world, hardly any of the emails that come to your business should make it to your inbox.

Leverage technology

There is a lot of wonderful technology available these days that can make your life a lot simpler and more organised. We use various software tools, such as budget planners, planning software and so on.

Budget planners can be especially useful when you're with a client, because they can demonstrate how they actually need to set aside a relatively small amount of money towards protecting their overall situation. These pieces of software will help them to visualise what it would look like to spend 2-3% of their take-home pay on an emergency fund, for example.

Leverage technology in any way you can to make sure that your diary is controlled and that your time is used effectively.

Creative communication

In this line of work, sometimes you have to tell people things that they might not want to hear. If you have a client who's significantly overweight, for instance, you might not be able to get them critical illness cover. Or their life insurance premiums might be really high. Having time before meetings can help you think of creative ways to break what could be perceived as bad news.

However you decide to communicate bad news to people, you have to do it with a smile and show your client that it's coming from a place of concern and honesty. You can't escape the fact that someone who's obese and in poor health will have to pay more for life insurance than someone who's in good shape and really fit. You can explain that changing some of their lifestyle habits could improve their health, and therefore lower their life insurance premium. But you have to do this in a sensitive way, and always from a place of concern. If your client knows that you mean well, they'll take that kind of news much better.

Chapter 7: There Should Always Be Time for Beer

Watch your spare time

It can be easy to have big, hairy, audacious goals and that's great, but what you have to ask yourself is, if achieving these big, hairy, audacious goals is at the detriment of your personal life then what's the point?

When you're putting all of your focus on building a business and working hard, your personal relationships will suffer. They deteriorate over time. You see it all the time, with business people who are on their second, third or even fourth marriage.

It doesn't wash when you go home to your spouse after barely seeing them and say, 'But I did it all for you.'

If you're completely honest with yourself, you didn't do all of these things for your partner, you did them for yourself. You're the only person who gets recognition for achieving your goals. You're the only person who sees the business growing and sees the money coming in. You're the one whose name goes on any awards you win. You're the only one who reaps the benefits of going to overseas conventions. Ultimately, all that you achieve comes back to you, the adviser.

When you fail to make time for your family and personal relationships, you will suddenly realise one day that your marriage is over (if it wasn't already), that your kids have grown up and you barely had any input into their development, and that you're suddenly in a lonely place.

I learned this lesson the hard way. My first marriage ended when my children were aged five and three. I was working hard all the time and I wasn't making time for them or my ex-wife. My ex-wife was working hard at the local pub. In fact, she met her future husband in that pub. So, the lesson here is that there should always be time for beer, preferably with your wife or other half. I'm not telling you this story with any bitterness attached to it. But it is important to recognise the impact that failing to make quality time for your family has on your relationships.

Finding space for quality time

We all live increasingly busy lives and it can sometimes feel like a challenge to make quality time for your loved ones. You feel as though your schedule is already full.

There's a famous story that perfectly illustrates this point and I'm sure it's one that you've probably heard before.

A philosophy professor stood in front of his students with an empty jar and a bottle of beer, and proceeded to fill the jar with rocks. 'Is the jar full?' he asked them when he finished, to which they replied, 'Yes.' Next, he took small pebbles and put them in the jar, giving it a small shake to allow them to slip between the larger rocks. Once again he asked the question, 'Is the jar full?' Once again, the students in his class said, 'Yes.' Finally, he took sand and poured it into the jar. Of course, the grains of sand found their way between the rocks and pebbles. When he'd finished, he asked the question again, 'Is the jar full?' and again his students said, 'Yes.'

He then explained that the jar represents your life, and the items he'd placed in it represent the different things that you spend your time and energy on: the rocks represent the important things that have real value, such as your family, your partner, your health, your children; the pebbles represent the other things that matter, such as your job, house, car, clothes and so forth; and the sand represents everything else, all the small stuff.

If you fill your time up with small stuff, the sand, you will not be able to fit the rocks and pebbles into your life.

One of the students asked about the beer. The professor opened the beer, smiled and poured it into the jar, stating that it didn't matter how full your life was, there was always room for a beer.

The point is that you find a balance between working and spending time with the people you love, whoever they may be.

You might have to spend some time working hard now, and when you're scraping by it can be virtually impossible to treat yourself and your family to nice things that you otherwise might enjoy, like a nice bottle of wine or a meal out, but you have to make sure you make provisions for rewards in the future.

There needs to be a demonstrable benefit to you having to work four weekends in a row, for example. So, if you have to work four weekends in a row, tell your partner that you'll go away for a weekend as soon as those four weeks are up. You also have to make sure you follow through on these rewards and don't make promises you can't keep.

You don't have to be available 24/7

When you're an entrepreneur with your own business, it can be difficult to switch off. As an employee it's easy; you go to work, you do your hours and you go home. You don't have the same emotional attachment and personal connection that you do when you own a business.

I believe that one of the big problems is that we, as business owners, have this notion that we need to be available 24/7, and that's absolutely not true. I was recently at a conference and some people were shocked when I handed them my business card and they saw that it didn't have my mobile phone number on it. They asked me how people got hold of me and I told them that, well, they don't. I have a PA system in place (that I'll talk more about later), and they can email me.

But what you have to remember is that people will often message you because they think something is urgent when, in reality, it could certainly wait, and it definitely doesn't need to be done at 6pm on a Saturday evening. For example, in the past, I could get a phone call or email from a client on a Saturday telling me that they desperately need their mortgage offer; should I send it to them? The answer is no. What are they going to do with it on a Saturday evening? The next step after I send their mortgage offer is for them to pass it on to their solicitor. Is the solicitor going to be working on a Saturday night? No. Do they have a mobile number for them? Of course not.

The point is that, while you could argue that many of us are in a service industry and should therefore respond to clients, you have to manage their expectations. I'm not a brain surgeon. Nothing I do is a matter of life and death. That means a client can wait until Monday morning to hear from me if they get in touch over the weekend.

I have a separate work phone, which I turn off at 5pm every Friday. There's no point in being at everyone's beck and call when the other links in the chain aren't at everyone's beck and call. You need to make sure you're spending quality time with your family and loved ones, which means you can't put work first seven days of the week.

Ask why people want something now

It can be very easy for clients to call you and tell you that they need their mortgage offer, for example, right now. It's worth exploring why they feel that there's such a sense of urgency, because more often than not this sense of urgency is misplaced.

When you ask a client why they need their mortgage offer now, often they'll tell you it's because the estate agent has been asking for it. But if you get in touch with their solicitor and ask if you got the mortgage offer to them, would they be in a position to exchange contracts, the answer is usually, 'No, we're weeks away from exchanging contracts.' In fact, if you speak to the solicitor you might discover that they're still waiting for the vendor to respond to their initial enquiries.

Once you have this information, you can go back to the client and tell them that, rather than hassling you for the mortgage offer, the estate agent should be hassling the vendor to send back the initial enquiries. The point of this example is that you need to have factually correct information for your clients.

When you know the situation, you can go back to them and explain why you're not going to rush to get them their mortgage offer. As long as you tell people why you're doing things with a smile and make sure that what you're telling them is factually correct, you can manage their expectations and avoid a lot of hassle for yourself in the process.

Upholding your boundaries

It's all well and good setting boundaries, like my decision to turn my work mobile off at 5pm on a Friday, but you have to make sure that once you set boundaries you uphold them.

I've made the mistake of letting my boundaries slip, and it's cost me. For instance, I don't usually work Fridays, but in the past I've let my guard down and answered the office phone when it rings. Usually, the response I get from my client is, 'Oh, I didn't think you worked Fridays, I was just going to leave a message with your answering service.' At that point, I'm quietly cursing myself for answering the phone, because my clients don't expect me to be there and I need to stick to the boundaries that I put in place.

Fundamentally this is about time protectionism. Protecting your time, both when you're at work and when you're not. One of the best things that I spend money on at my business is a service called All Day PA (other virtual assistants are available). What they do is answer my phones and take messages. That means whenever someone calls my business, day or night, weekday or weekend, the phone is answered by an actual person.

They take a message and then email me, and I can then decide whether I or one of my team need to respond to that query or not. It costs me an average of £30 a month and I'd say it's the best piece of time protectionism there is.

Plan your spare time

It can be incredibly easy to let spare time drift. We've all done it, where we've got to the end of the weekend and don't really know how we spent the last two days. The key to avoiding this scenario is to plan your spare time as much as you plan your work time.

When I say spare time, I'm talking about any time that you're not at work – that's evenings, weekends and holidays. This principle of planning your spare time to the same degree that you plan your work time comes from the Strategic Coach® Program. I'm not saying that this is an easy thing to do necessarily. But in a perfect world, you should plan something positive to do on the weekends and in the evenings.

What that is will depend on you and your partner, and your kids if you have them. You need to make sure you're planning time with your other half. Of course, if you're single you can do whatever you want in your spare time, but if you're in a relationship and/or have a family, then you need to consider what they'll want to do too. Have a meeting with your partner and kids. Talk about what you'd all like to do and share the plan that you come up with.

I remember once hearing a story about a man whose kids would prepare his golf clubs for him every Saturday morning and send him off to play a round of golf because if he didn't play golf, he was a miserable bugger for the whole weekend. The kids worked out that if their dad had played golf, he was a much happier person to be with for the rest of the weekend. That just means that his round of golf would have been part of the plan for their weekend, every week.

This book is all about how your goals can come true, but it's important to remember that the goals you write for your personal life and your spare time are just as important as the ones you write for your business. Don't neglect them, and remember, there's always time for beer.

Chapter 8: 'If You're Going Through Hell...

"Keep Going!"

This is a quote that's famously attributed to Winston Churchill during the Second World War (there is no guarantee he actually said the quote, but the sentiment stands regardless). It stems from the idea that Hell is certainly not a place where you want to stop. But it's also about the concept that the only way to get out of whatever Hell you're experiencing is to just keep going, to keep pushing.

While it might have been said in the context of war, where there could be bullets flying past you and bombs going off, it's applicable to anyone who runs their own business too. You might not be in physical danger, but that doesn't mean you aren't under immense pressure. There are countless stories of people who hit a rough patch and just give up, only to later discover they were just metres away from that gold seam that would have changed their lives. You don't want to be one of the people who just gives in.

Why did I keep going?

This is a topic that's very close to my heart, because I've been through some very difficult times and I've come out the other side by keeping going.

In 2010, I was on the edge of bankruptcy. And now, ten years later, I'm a millionaire. All because I kept going. I'm proof that this mindset works. I established my business, DB Financial, in June 2006. In November 2006, my mum passed away, and 12 weeks later, in February 2007, my dad also died. I'd been so busy setting up my business that I hadn't seen either of them as much as I would have liked to at that time. It's still one of my biggest regrets.

When my parents passed away, I received an inheritance and Bonnie and I used that to buy a bigger house. We had a big mortgage and we kept our other house and rented it to a friend. Not long after we'd moved, towards the end of 2007, the market for mortgages dried up. It was the beginning of the global financial crisis that took hold in 2008.

As I mentioned in Chapter 5, before the crash, I was arranging 15 to 20 mortgages per month, which gave me a pretty decent income. In 2008, I arranged just 25 mortgages in the whole year. This period was really scary. We had a big mortgage and other debts. We were borrowing from Peter to pay Paul and we became trapped in the debt spiral. In 2010, I decided to seek help to make our financial situation more manageable.

In the midst of all of this, it would have been very easy for me to walk away from my business. But I didn't and there were two big reasons why. Firstly, I didn't want to let Bonnie down. She had put a lot of time and energy into the business, and I wanted to make a success of it to give us both the lifestyle that we wanted.

Secondly, I wanted to make my mum proud. When I was a child, my dad had worked for the Armed Forces, which meant we moved around a lot. All of our moves were timed around my schooling, so that I'd have security and stability in my education at key points. I have a brother who's a year younger than me, but all of our moves were arranged for me to be able to do my O Levels and my A Levels with minimal disruption, as I was the brighter of the two of us (well that's what I tell myself!).

When I was younger, my mum wanted me to be the chairman of Imperial Chemical Industries (ICI), which at that stage was the largest manufacturing company in the UK. ICI was bought out and disbanded in 2008, but when I was growing up it was one of the biggest businesses in Britain. In the 1980s, John Harvey-Jones was the chairman; he was like that generation's Peter Jones, and my mum's goal was for me to be as successful as him.

Until I set up my own business in 2006, I'd been involved in various partnerships. But setting up DB Financial was a really big and important step for me. I wanted to make my mum proud, and so giving up just wasn't an option. Even during the most challenging times, I wouldn't have considered giving up my business. If you're going through Hell, keep going.

How did I keep going?

Having the desire to keep going is important, but that alone won't get you through tough times. I took a number of practical steps that allowed me and Bonnie to avoid bankruptcy and to keep my business going.

In 2010, I realised that I needed help to manage my debt and financial situation. I reorganised our outgoings into a more manageable monthly payment. Bonnie and I also made sacrifices to help bring in some extra money. Our house is just a short drive from Gatwick Airport, so we rented out our driveway to people who were going away. We also rented two of the rooms in our house to pilots who were training at the easyJet training centre nearby. For most of this period, we were just doing what we had to in order to make ends meet.

Renting out rooms to people we didn't know didn't always go smoothly either. I remember one woman who lived with us, we'll call her Sally, who didn't really fit in. I was the one who'd agreed for her to stay with us. And I remember one evening that we had some friends round and I said that it was just typical that the one time I choose someone to move in they're a 'loony nutter', and that it doesn't happen to Bonnie, she just gets these nice handsome pilots.

Anyway, I hadn't realised that Sally had come home and was sitting at the bottom of the stairs. She heard everything I said. She even tried to call me to tell me that she could hear me, but my phone was on the mantelpiece and I didn't hear it ringing. The next morning, she confronted me about it and asked me to apologise. I told her I wasn't sorry that I'd said it, but that I was sorry she'd heard. Of course, not long afterwards she moved out.

But when she did move out, she kept hold of our key. I had kept £50 of her deposit to pay to repaint her room because she'd put posters up on the walls and the blu tac had ruined the paint. We had an argument over that because she said she'd come and repaint the room herself if that was the problem, and I had to explain that keeping our key wasn't the equivalent of me taking £50 to pay for some decent paint to redecorate her room. In the end, she returned the key, but that's just an example of the additional stress we went through during that time.

Having lodgers and sharing your home like that is far from ideal, and it's particularly difficult when you're already on edge because there's no money around and you're having to be careful.

Financially, we were also renting out our old house, which was generating a bit more income. However, we were renting it to a friend initially, for about £900 a month. When our friend moved out after five years and we put it up for let on the open market, we were able to get £1,350 a month for the property. With hindsight, that extra money would have been incredibly useful and would have made a difference to us, but it was rented to a friend and well looked after. The new higher rent didn't always come in on time as we didn't really know the new tenant. This added more stress when we could have done without it.

The other thing that kept me going was having a dog that I could take out for walks. The dog really was a lifesaver because it meant we went out for walks and had a bit of distraction. Walking the dog also allowed us to meet some of our neighbours, whom we became friends with and whom we could have round for dinner, or go to their houses (which also meant we could avoid going out to restaurants and the costs involved with that). Having that sense of community also helped in those difficult times.

E + R = O

This formula is what I aspire to live by. **E**vent + **R**eaction = **O**utcome. This comes from the idea that events happen and you can't control the events. However, what you can control, in fact all you can control, is your reaction to the events. How you react to the events in your life will determine the outcome.

So, if you have a negative reaction to an event, you're more likely to get a negative outcome. If, on the other hand, you have a positive reaction to an event, you're more likely to get a positive outcome. There are no guarantees, but by reacting in a positive way you're increasing the chances of seeing a positive outcome, and the same holds true if you react negatively.

I don't remember where I first heard about this formula, I have a feeling that I have Jack Canfield to thank for it, but it's a great approach to life, and it's one that I've carried around and tried to live by for over 20 years.

Knowing when to ask for help

As I mentioned, in 2010 I got some help with my financial affairs because I realised I couldn't manage everything on my own. Knowing when to ask for help, and not being afraid to reach out, is essential when you're going through difficult periods of your life. It's also important to reciprocate and help others when you can – I believe in the old adage of 'givers gain'.

There are two sides to this: asking for help with your business, and just being there for people when they need support as a friend. I'm a big believer in giving support to people where you can. I've seen it from both sides of the coin. You heard from Michelle Hoskin at the start of the book about how she's guided me and supported me at various points since I've known her. You've also heard Sarah's story and learned how I supported her when she reached out.

The key is that this support, whichever way it's going, has come from genuine relationships. They're friendships that I've formed over the years and I believe that when you're authentic and genuine, you attract authentic and genuine people to you. I've taken help and support from people and then I've paid it back down the chain. I know that people like Sarah will do the same thing when they're able to.

Don't get me wrong though, I've also worked with my share of people who weren't authentic or genuine. There's one example that specifically comes to mind, of an old business partner of mine who ripped me off to the tune of about £50,000–£60,000.

I hadn't heard from him for a few years, when he got in touch out of the blue and said that he needed to meet up with me. When I asked why, he told me that he was my new business development manager (BDM) for a large life assurance company, and he would like to showcase their products. I didn't take any joy in the fact that he'd ripped me off and now he'd had to come to me because he needed my business. But I did go and meet him because I wanted to find out how his life had changed for the worse. I can honestly say that in the whole time he was my BDM, I never bought a policy from him for one of my clients. There was no chance I was going to give him any help.

The need for integrity

What my old business partner didn't have was integrity. He didn't think ahead and realise that his decision to rip me off by tens of thousands of pounds would come back to hurt him in the end. In this business, and any business, you need to have a long-term interest in your clients and you need to operate with integrity.

I'm also a big believer in the fact that you have to practise what you preach as a financial adviser. It's no good me sitting in front of a client telling them that they need XYZ's worth of life insurance if I don't have the appropriate level of insurance for myself. You have to make sure that you're congruent with the advice you give people.

In fact, when I sought help to rearrange my debts and put all the paperwork together, I was told that I needed to reduce my life insurance coverage. At that time I had critical illness cover, which was sufficient to pay my mortgage, and so I was paying a small fortune in life insurance premiums. This wasn't something I was prepared to give up though, so I agreed to reduce the level of cover to reduce the premium for my budget, but I never did reduce the level of cover I had in place.

I believe that's really important, because if you've got enough life insurance, critical illness and income protection cover then you can sell with integrity to others.

Developing your inner resources

While there are practical things you can do when you're going through Hell to keep you going, like those I've discussed in this chapter and elements earlier in the book such as budgeting and income, there are also inner resources that you need to cultivate to keep pushing.

You need to have confidence, resilience and a degree of arrogance. I'd say that I'm arrogant, but not in the extreme. So, I have strong opinions about things and I'm willing to change my opinion, but you need to have a very compelling argument if you're going to convince me that I'm wrong.

It's also essential to have confidence and belief in yourself. I'm convinced that the only person you need to believe in is yourself, you don't need to believe in anyone else. I really do think it's that simple: believe in yourself. You will take a battering along the way and you'll encounter people who don't like your attitude or what you've got to say, but provided this comes from a place of love and the genuine belief that what you're doing is right, you'll become unstoppable.

This isn't about being single minded and looking inward. It's about connecting with the world around you, recognising who needs you and who's around you and supporting you, and being able to tap into that part of you that allows you to act from a position of love. It's like I said earlier in the chapter, if you help other people and accept help from others, you create a chain that passes the good on.

Authenticity is everything

One of the most important things I've learned is that you have to be authentic in everything you do. I've also learned that if you're authentic you don't have to work too hard. If you're just being yourself it's the easiest thing in the world because you're just being who you are. You're not putting up a front or pretending to be something you're not. You're you. Having that authenticity makes everything easier.

But it's also essential in this line of work. Fundamentally, our job as financial advisers is to help people find the courage and give them the confidence to take care of their families. That's all we need to do. There are so many people in this line of work who try to trick people, or confuse them with charts, but that's not the way to go about it.

If you're authentic, honest, passionate and have belief in both yourself and what you do then that will come through to clients. If you behave like that, you'll end up with clients who stay with you for decades because they know that you'll give them honest answers to their questions.

I have clients who say, 'Oh no, we've got our annual review with Doug, which means he's going to give us a hard time about the fact that we're still overspending. Can we defer it for three months so we've got time to tidy up our bank statements?' Of course I won't let them defer their reviews, but they know that the reason I give them a hard time is because I care. It's because I want them to do the right things to secure their future. My clients know that and they want me to be honest with them because it shows them that I care about them.

It comes back to the need to have integrity. When you have integrity, honesty follows. I'd say in our line of work as financial advisers, integrity is essential. There's no place in this business for people who are just looking to rip their clients off. You need to have integrity at your core.

This integrity will help you when you're going through Hell. It's how you calibrate your internal compass, if you like. We all have gut feelings about situations and those come from our core – our integrity helps us to see opportunities. Of course, we've all done things that when we look back, we realise weren't a good idea. Hindsight is a wonderful thing. But the general rule is to trust your gut feeling and if something sounds too good to be true, it's not a good idea.

When you have integrity and are authentic, you attract other people who are like you. This gives you an invaluable support network when you are going through tough times.

We all know people who fly into a job, sell, sell, sell, sell and then two years later you hear that they're doing the same thing, but in a completely different sector. These people don't have integrity. They're not working in financial services because they genuinely want to help people.

I would describe this profession as a calling. If you go into it because you genuinely want to help and do the right thing, you can make a fantastic amount of money without ever sacrificing your integrity.

Chapter 9: The Cost of Loyalty

Mercedes vs BMW

'You will get all you want in life if you help enough other people get what they want.' – Zig Ziglar

That quote sums up what I'm going to talk about in this chapter. I've also got a personal story that explains the cost of loyalty.

In all of my goals that I've written down, I've always said I drive a Mercedes. It might be this Mercedes or that Mercedes, but while the model changes over the years the brand doesn't. But the funny thing is that I actually drive a BMW.

The reason for that is very simple. A good friend of mine, Mario, is a car salesman for BMW. I want to support him, so I went to his dealership and bought a BMW. Although I did this to support him, the irony is that he gave me such a good deal he didn't end up making any money on it. His sales director even asked him how much money he thought he'd made on the sale to me. Mario guessed it was about £1,000, but it was actually just £100. By the time he'd filled up the fuel tank and thrown in a couple of other extras, he didn't make any money on that sale at all, so he just got credit for it and didn't make any money off it.

That was a few years ago. More recently, I decided to swap the BMW I bought originally for a new one, because the one I had was a little bit low and uncomfortable to drive (I must be getting OLD). This time I told Mario that, while I appreciated him getting me an amazing deal, he couldn't do that again. He had to make sure he made some money on the sale.

So, despite the fact that in all of my goal lists I drive a Mercedes, my last two cars have been BMWs, and that's the cost of loyalty. Sometimes you forgo the things that you want for a friend or to help someone else out.

It's not a cost, it's an investment

I call it a cost, but I do that in an ironic way. I don't see it as a cost, I see it as an investment. In fact, everything, one way or another, is an investment. It might be an investment for some peace of mind. It might be an investment in a nice feeling. It might be an investment in somebody else. It's a cost that you should pay, it's worthwhile, but really, if you think of it as an investment then it ceases to be a cost at all.

Coming back to the story about me choosing BMW over a Mercedes, it's important to remember that driving a Mercedes has been on my list of goals for years. It's something that I've visualised many times. I even had a Mercedes at one point before life became difficult financially. This goal has motivated me to work hard. But in spite of all of that, driving a BMW rather than a Mercedes is a sacrifice I've been willing to make because it fits in with my core belief in loyalty.

Remember the chapter where I talked about SMART goals? If your goal isn't SMART (specific, measurable, achievable, realistic, trackable) you change it. Even though driving a Mercedes fits all the criteria for a SMART goal, it doesn't fit in with my beliefs around loyalty. For now, I've chosen to drive a BMW. If Mario ever moves to Mercedes, I'll have my opportunity to own a Mercedes and go back to my original goal.

How loyalty helps in business

I've talked about a few core qualities that you need in order to succeed in this business, such as integrity and authenticity in the previous chapter. Loyalty is one of those core qualities too.

Loyalty leads to longevity. I can tell you that with certainty. I have clients who have been with me for 20, 25, even 30 years. The reason they're loyal to me is because I'm loyal to them. That means you need to be honest with them and have integrity in what you're saying; that breeds loyalty. What you have to remember is that what you put out into the world comes back in spades.

At the time of writing, I'm in the process of changing the way I do business. I'm moving to a new environment and my clients are moving with me. It hasn't been a difficult transition because they're loyal to me and I'm loyal to them. They trust me when I explain what I'm doing and why, which is why so many of them are coming with me.

Build relationships with loyalty

There are plenty of examples of people who aren't loyal to their clients, but that often means their clients aren't loyal to them. You can't trust people who are fickle and who behave without integrity and loyalty.

When someone reaches out to connect with me on LinkedIn, for example, I'll always have a look to see who they are and what connections we have in common. If I accept a connection from someone and within 30 seconds I receive a message telling me what they can do for me, I've turned off. They've made it transactional. They haven't tried to build a relationship with me, or a lasting connection. They're only interested in selling and, to me, that's boring.

When you look at their profile, they'll most likely have had ten jobs in the last 15 years. A year here, a couple of years there and so on. They don't stick to anything because they get people on board and then they move on. To be fair, some people might move around so much because they're looking for the right thing. But more often than not, they're sales people jumping from one place to another, and when I see that I always take anything they say to me with a pinch of salt.

If anyone is struggling with this, first and foremost I'd say that it means you haven't found your calling or the right fit. I'm in the protection arena of financial services – life insurance, income protection insurance and so on. I'd say that this is one of the only financial services businesses where, if you do the right thing with care for the products you're selling and the people you're selling to, you can't sell too much. No widow has ever complained because her husband had too much life insurance.

Loyalty doesn't cost you a thing

Loyalty, like the other core internal qualities I've talked about of integrity, authenticity and honesty, doesn't cost you any money. But they are all invaluable tools that can help you and help the people around you.

The main point I'm making in this chapter is that you need to focus on your internal qualities first. Work on what's inside and apply those core qualities to your life. If you do that, then you'll find that the external things you're looking for – like a Mercedes – will come to you. Sometimes they might be in the form of a BMW though.

Think of that quote from Zig Ziglar at the start of this chapter: 'You will get all you want in life if you help enough other people get what they want.' It's as simple as that.

Chapter 10: You Fat B*stard!

Being fit for purpose

I want to start by clarifying that I'm the fat b*stard this chapter refers to. It's something that I'm working on because I know how important it is to stay healthy. If you think that you're a fat b*stard too then this chapter will be especially important. Even if you don't class yourself in that group, there are still some important lessons to learn about looking after yourself.

Improving my health and fitness all began when I started with the new firm in Egham nearly 20 years ago, and I was commuting there from Redhill. This was when they were widening the M25 to make it four/five lanes, so there were a lot of roadworks. That meant it could take anywhere from 45 minutes to three hours to get to work.

To avoid the traffic, I started going to work really, really early. I'd get to the office and be the only person there. Opposite the office was a gym. I decided that, rather than getting in early and starting work, I might as well pop to the gym and at least I could use their showers etc. after a workout, and so on.

The first day I went in there, I ran about 100m on the treadmill and I was ready to throw up. I was so unfit. I spent a lot of time in the car. We lived close to a McDonalds, a chip shop, a Beefeater – it was easy to walk to these places, pick up a takeaway and eat it at home. It's easy to see why I wasn't the peak of physical fitness.

At that time of day, I was the only person in the gym, apart from the owner Karen, who used to train early in the morning. She helped me with my training and, 18 months later, I completed the London Marathon. I don't tell people that I ran the London Marathon, because I walked some of it, but I got my medal and that was one of the goals that was on my list.

I'd like to add that I didn't feel ready when I stepped up to the starting line. The furthest I'd run before the marathon was 15 miles, because that's all I'd had time to train for. In actual fact, I missed out on the ballot initially and felt quite relieved, only for a friend who worked for the marathon to offer me a space. I couldn't say no, so that was it, I was in, no turning back.

I found myself with the thousands of other runners, and several hours and one missing toenail later, I'd completed the course. The support you get from the crowd on the way round is really what keeps you going. If you're going to run the London Marathon, make sure you've got your name in big letters on the front and back of your shirt so people can cheer you on, it gives you a real boost.

My point isn't that you should go to the gym and start training for a marathon. My point is that you should get some support. It doesn't matter what the goal is, but I think you should always find that support wherever it might come from.

Back to being a fat b*stard, and my support network as I try to lose weight comes from the 'Gut Busters'. We're three guys, all in our mid-50s, and each week we check in with our weight and BMI and, of course, there's a bit of banter along the way.

Personally, I need something to aim for and look forward to – like completing the London Marathon or trekking up Kilimanjaro. This year, we've decided we're going to complete the Three Peaks Challenge. Most of the guys who are signing up aren't particularly fit, so instead of climbing Snowdon, Scafell Pike and Ben Nevis in 24 hours, we're giving ourselves 36 hours.

Remember that your goals always need to be achievable, and if they're not you change them. That's what we've done here, by giving ourselves a little bit longer. This isn't about being the best, or the fastest, this is about giving yourself a goal that you feel you can achieve.

Why is your fitness important?

There are three main reasons why it's important to stay in shape, and especially if, like me, you're someone who deals with life insurance, critical illness cover and income protection.

Firstly, when we're visiting clients, we're trying to give them the confidence to make decisions about their future. We're protecting their future by helping them arrange the likes of life insurance, critical illness cover and income protection. Our aim is to put them in a position where they know that, if anything were to happen to them, their family would be ok.

To me, it seems rather ironic if you turn up to a meeting and you're overweight, out of breath, sweating, but you're there to talk to them about their health. How is that conducive to convincing someone that they ought to do the right thing by their family?

Secondly, these conversations with clients revolve around their goals, their aspirations and their life. You're trying to convince them that you want to be with them in the long term on their journey as they prepare for the future. But how can you convince them that you'll be with them in the long term if you look like you might have a heart attack and drop dead at any second?

Finally, how you look after yourself and your immediate environment reflects on a lot of other areas of a person's life. You've got to think about how you come across to potential clients. If you take care of your health and fitness, that indicates that you take care of other aspects of your life, and therefore your client will believe that you're going to take care of them.

Remember that people tend to care more about themselves than about other people. As a result, if you don't appear to care about yourself, it might suggest you'll care less about others.

Finding time to get fit

In our profession, we spend a lot of time sitting in front of a computer, sitting in meetings with clients, and sitting in cars or on trains going to meetings with clients. If you want to lose weight and/or improve your fitness, you need to make time for it.

That means putting it in your diary. It has to be a non-negotiable part of your week. I'm the first to admit that I'm not perfect, but I'm working on it and without dedicating a bit of time to my fitness, I'd easily be obese.

How to talk to clients who are overweight

We all know that being overweight or obese is a risk factor for a whole range of illnesses and conditions. When you're arranging life insurance, critical illness cover or income protection insurance, this is certainly something that's going to come into play.

When you have a client who's overweight, this can be a difficult topic to broach. I'd like to tell you how I handled this with one client in particular.

This was a young lady who was looking for life insurance and critical illness cover. She was around 5'6" to 5'7" tall and I'd say she weighed somewhere between 18 and 20 stone. You already know at this point that she's going to have a high BMI and this is one of the indicators as to whether the life insurance company will consider them.

We hadn't given her a quote at this point, but we had managed to find a company that was prepared to give her life insurance. But they wouldn't give her critical illness cover. I was surprised we'd managed to find life insurance, so I called her and this is what I said, 'I've got some brilliant news. We've gone through the charts of the various life insurance companies and, for most of them, you're just not tall enough for their charts.'

I paused, and then she said, 'Doug, have you just found a really kind way of saying that I'm fat?'

My response was, 'Well, you could say that, but I couldn't possibly comment [said with a grin in my voice]. However, as far as the charts are concerned, there's one that's prepared to arrange life insurance for you, which is amazing. However, they're not going to give you critical illness cover because they felt that there's too high a risk, as you can probably imagine. But I know you're working on your weight, so this is something that we can look at again in the future and if the situation improves we can apply again.'

The most important thing was, though, that we'd got her life insurance cover, so if she were to die prematurely, her boyfriend would be able to pay the mortgage off.

I also told her, 'The thing to bear in mind is that we've managed to get your boyfriend life insurance and critical illness cover, because he is tall enough.'

She was all for him having the cover, but sometimes we encounter a situation where someone says that, if they can't get cover, they don't want their partner to have it either. The way I handle this scenario is by mentioning it before they have a chance to. Essentially I'm handling the objection before it comes up from the client. Oftentimes, when you approach it this way, the response is that their partner should have full cover, even if they can't.

Honesty over diplomacy

You have to develop a sense of humour when you're in this line of work. I also find that it's much more effective to be honest and truthful with people from the outset. I often start a conversation with a client by saying, 'Look, we need to agree that I'm going to be honest with you rather than diplomatic, is that ok?'

They usually reply, 'Yes, of course that is.' And my response is, 'Great, because if I'm honest with you it's so much quicker than having to be diplomatic.'

There are all kinds of nuances with life insurance, as you may well know. One that comes up frequently is Waiver of Contribution. This means that the insurance company will pay your life and critical illness cover premiums for you if you're off sick for more than six months. It's essentially an insurance policy within an insurance policy.

Most people aren't even aware that they could have this policy, but in order to get it, you have to be in perfect health. Despite being unaware of this policy initially, if you apply for it and your client is rejected, they often get angry about this, because they feel as though something is being taken away from them.

This is why it's so important to ask your clients to fill in a medical questionnaire before you quote for their cover. That way, you can look at what's on there and manage expectations. You can tell them that you'll be able to get cover for X, Y and Z, but explain that there's a chance they might not get it for A or B. You handle the problem before it becomes a problem.

There's no expiry date on your birth certificate

Let's not beat about the bush, life insurance is a depressing topic to talk about. A lot of people don't like facing their own mortality, but that's exactly what you're asking them to do when you're arranging this kind of cover.

You have to make it easy for them to do that. The way I approach this is to say to them, 'Imagine that you died last week...' I always kill my clients off the week before I see them, because if I kill them off next week, it feels like I'm tempting fate when I'm writing up a life insurance policy for them.

But this gives me a good opening to start talking to them about what they wanted to achieve before they died, as well as what they wanted to happen to their family after this happened. You have to ask these difficult questions, but then I find it's best to leave them out there. Let them consider the answers.

While it's understandable that people don't like to think about these things, the fact of the matter is that you have to. There's no expiry date on your birth certificate, we don't know what's going to happen. The best we can do is imagine that it's already happened and work backwards from there to make sure our clients' families and loved ones are taken care of.

If you come across a client who tells you they don't care what happens to their wife and kids if they die, you've got to question whether they're the kind of person you want as a client.

You've always got to reflect on who you have as clients. If you can't get them underwritten for insurance, having them as a client doesn't make you any money. You need to find people who are prepared to let you take a different approach if that's what's required to find them cover.

Being healthy, what's the worst that could happen?

If you ignore everything else you've read in this book, but just go away and work on becoming fitter and healthier, I'd say that would put you in the top 25% of the financial advice profession.

There's nothing wrong with being as healthy as you can be. Let's approach this from a different perspective. Even if you're totally healthy, there's still a one in two chance that you'll get cancer at some point in your life. So, why compound those odds by increasing your chances with heart disease, type 2 diabetes, or stroke by being overweight?

If this chapter has offended you then I'm sorry to say that it's probably because it's talking about something you need to hear. Becoming overweight is something that can creep up on you. It's also something that people don't like to bring to your attention. But I'm here to tell you that it's something you should address. It's important and, really, there are no downsides to becoming healthier. You need to lead by example and show your clients that you practise what you preach. So, if you're not tall enough for the BMI charts, maybe it's time to do something about it!

Chapter 11: All You Need Is Love

Ok how to go the extra mile
in 100 yards

There can be a lot of expectations around love. The concept of a soul mate, the only person for you. The idea of your eyes meeting across a crowded room and instantly falling in love. I suppose that can happen. But in my experience it's more often the case that you connect with someone and then love comes, but you have to work at it.

I would say that love has played an unquestionable role in my journey to success. But I've had to work at it. Take my marriage as an example. I have the most wonderful wife. But one of my goals has always been to be happily married to Bonnie. As I've already explained, writing goals doesn't have to be something you do every single day, but it does have to be something you do consistently. Your goals always need to be in the present tense.

Being happily married to Bonnie is a goal that I've been writing for years. And it's true. I am happily married to Bonnie. For me, there are two ways of looking at this goal. One is that it's a reminder that I am happily married, and that can be useful when you're going through a difficult time. The other way of looking at that goal is as an instruction. Remember the principle of E + R = O (Event + Reaction = Outcome)? This instruction that you're happily married can help you choose a reaction to an event. If you've told yourself that you're happily married to someone, your reaction to an event is likely to be different than if you don't feel happy in your marriage.

I'm not saying that this is easy. Long-term relationships require work. Sometimes it's hard work and sometimes it's easy work, but either way it's something that you have to constantly work at.

Relationships are 100/100

People often say that a relationship should be 50/50, but I don't think that's right. If you're only prepared to give 50%, it's never going to work. A relationship should be 100/100, you have to give 100% if you want it to work.

Of course, it's not possible to always give 100%. Sometimes you'll be giving your 100% and your other half might only be giving 50%, and at other points it will be the other way around. But the point is that if you love somebody, you'll work your way towards giving 100% as often as you possibly can. Sometimes we need to remind ourselves of that, which is why having 'being happily married' can be a very useful goal.

While you should always be striving to hit that 100%, you should also know that you're never going to get there because nobody is perfect. There will always be something nibbling away at it, but it's about progress not perfection.

Don't bail on love

There's no doubt about it, relationships can be hard, but that doesn't mean you should bail out of them as soon as things start to get rough. Think back to Chapter 8: 'If you're going through Hell, keep going.' Relationships are the same. There will be hard times, but there will also be good times if you work at things.

My parents had their problems, but they stayed together through thick and thin. It's something that's always stuck with me. I know that there have been times in my and Bonnie's relationship when she or I could have said, 'Let's call this a day.' And sometimes it's understandable that you might feel that way, especially when things are rough, but you have to balance that out by remembering what attracted you to one another in the first place. I don't think you need to be soul mates to have a happy marriage and lasting relationship, but you do need to be tolerant. Nobody is perfect.

I also believe that love keeps going if you make a decision to keep it going. You have to make the effort to remain connected. If you become complacent, you can drift apart and before you know it, it becomes impossible to get back together. It really doesn't take long for a rift to open up, so love is something you have to keep working on.

How to stay connected

I can give you some practical tips on how to stay connected within a relationship. Firstly, you have to learn to bite your tongue. Secondly, write down all of the jobs that you're asked to do and make sure that you do them within six months. If you've been asked to do something three times, you should do it instantly. You might think I'm joking, but I genuinely have a list in my phone that's titled: 'Jobs for a happier Bonnie.'

The other thing I used to do, although I've had to stop because it winds Bonnie up, is ask which jobs are the most important, because there is only so much free time in a weekend. I don't want to have ten jobs on my list, get through eight of them but still be in the doghouse because the two I didn't do were actually the most important. I'm not a psychic, which is why it's so important to communicate.

You might think that this sounds a little trite or simplistic, but it's about making an effort and that's what love is.

It's also important to keep the romance alive. One of the best ways to do that is to go the extra mile when someone isn't expecting it. One of my top tips is to buy flowers every now and again. Don't do it every week, because then it becomes a habit and an expectation, but every now and again buy flowers. Don't just pop to your nearest garage either, go to Marks & Spencer. If you're going to make the grand gesture of buying flowers, buy quality. Spend £12 instead of £5.

Whenever I buy flowers for Bonnie, I go to Marks & Spencer. It's two miles away and it's not on my way home from the office, but I always go there to buy flowers. I don't just pop into the garage that's walking distance from my office. It takes a little extra effort and it makes all the difference. You just have to give your 100% with no expectation of getting 100% back.

As I was writing this book, someone mentioned a book by Gary Chapman called The Five Love Languages – turns out you could spend 25 years in a relationship speaking the wrong Love Language, or not spending quite enough time using the right one. You really do not want to do that...

According to Chapman, the five ways to express and experience these so-called 'love languages' are:

- Words of affirmation
- Quality time
- Giving gifts
- Acts of service
- Physical touch

If you have the feeling that you are not quite on the same wavelength with your spouse/significant other, check out this book. There is a good chance that you are speaking in your love language (how you would like to be treated) and your spouse is speaking to you in theirs, and it is not quite compatible.

Worth a look and it will go some way to you achieving your 100%.

Why do I do things out of love?

As I said earlier in the book, there are two people whom I do things for: Bonnie and my mum. I still do things for the love of my mum because it helps me to keep her alive. I learned a lot from her, my qualities like honesty, integrity and patience all came from her. She also taught me that you should just be yourself, you shouldn't be different people. Be you and you can't go far wrong.

I do things for the love of Bonnie because she honestly has no idea how great she is. She is so much more capable than she gives herself credit for. She struggles to believe in herself and she worries an awful lot about what other people think, but everyone who meets her loves her. Bonnie had a really hard upbringing, and she came out the other side. She so much deserves to be loved. It's no more or less than she deserves. While she infuriates me sometimes, and I'm sure I infuriate her, I always love her. I sometimes wish that if I could give her a little bit of my belief in her, she'd be even more incredible. I think I need to tell her that sometimes.

Helping others is an extension of love

For me, doing things from a place of love makes a positive difference to other people's lives. When I talk about helping other people, it doesn't always have to be a grand gesture. For example, I'm the kind of person who will collect up all of the glasses on our table and put them back on the bar before I leave a pub. There's no harm in it and it's only a small gesture, but these little things make a difference. Often I think that surely everybody behaves like this, but then I realise that they don't. And that's why making those small gestures does make a difference.

Let me give you an example. I was at a four-day conference (MDRT) in America in 2019. On the first day, I queued up with everyone else for coffee. When I got to the front of the queue, I started chatting to the barista while she made my coffee, who told me during this chat that she had a son. I had a couple of tiny koalas attached to my badge so I gave her one of them for her son. The following day I was in the same queue and when I got to the front the same barista served me. Her face lit up when she saw me, considerably more than it had for the 20–30 people she'd served ahead of me. There were 14,000 people at that conference. She greeted me with a smile and said, 'Hi, how are you today?' I responded, 'I'm great but how do you possibly remember me from yesterday?' She told me it was not only because I'd given her the koala for her son, but also because I was one of the only people she'd served who said please and thank you. I was flabbergasted.

I have another example from later at that same conference. I was in the hotel bar area when I heard the young waitress nearby give out a bit of a sigh. I asked if she was having a tough day and she turned to me and smiled. She had the prettiest face and was wearing barely any makeup and I told her so. It visibly lifted her spirits. Later that evening, I was looking for a nice glass of red wine at the bar, but as it wasn't the hotel I was staying in I was struggling to get served at that time of the evening as I had no cash and no room key. The waitress I'd seen earlier in the day spotted me and brought over the largest glass of red wine I've ever seen, at no charge. I think it's safe to say she wouldn't have done that had I not paid her a very simple compliment earlier in the day.

Why wouldn't you?

I know that some people think that I spoil my clients by going the extra mile, but my question is always, 'Why wouldn't you do that?'

Let me give you an example. One of my clients recently got in touch because she had moved some money around and wanted to make a withdrawal, but was having trouble filling in the form. She also told me that they wanted to see a bank statement and she couldn't work out how to print a bank statement from the online system. So, she gave me her online banking details (I would say that is incredibly trusting) so that I could go online and get her a statement. I did that and printed it out for her. Then I asked her what the other form was, so she sent that to me, I printed it, filled it out, addressed an envelope and put a stamp on it and drove over to give her the paperwork.

At the time of writing, many people in the UK are unable to leave their homes because they're self-isolating due to the Coronavirus pandemic. This client of mine falls into that group. I drove out to her home with the forms, all she had to do was sign them, hand them back to me and I popped them in the postbox.

Now, on my way over there, I'd stopped at a shop to pick up a couple of bits for Bonnie and myself, including a couple of packets of vegetables. While I was with this client, I asked her if she had any vegetables and she told me she hadn't been able to get hold of any and couldn't go out to the shops, so I gave her one of the packets that I'd just bought.

Some people would say, 'Why would you do all of that?' and my question to them is, 'Why wouldn't you do that?' You see, the extra mile isn't actually a mile, it just needs to be 100 yards, but to the person you're helping it will feel like a mile.

Conclusion

You have a lifetime of business wisdom in just one book, what do you plan to do with it? These are the key takeaways from the book, use them as a gentle reminder:

- Start by dealing with the simple things.

- Always trust your gut. If something just doesn't feel right then don't do it, because it will cost you in the long term.

- Always have integrity. It's one of your most valuable qualities. An ex-business partner of mine adopted the sales strategy 'taking your bite out of them before they take it out of you' but this is not a good long-term game plan.

- Be yourself. It's the easiest thing in the world.

- Believe in yourself. Sometimes it's the hardest thing in the world, but trust that by believing in yourself you'll find the strength and courage to achieve what you're aiming for.

- If you are in a relationship, it needs to be 100/100. Going 50/50 just doesn't cut it.

- If you are married – remember Winston and keep going!!!

On the next page is your first goals list. Write down at least ten goals and don't forget to write them in the present tense: I earn ...... I drive ..... I am happily.... I own..... I turn up 15 minutes before every appointment....

Then take a picture of your list and send it to doug@dougbennett.co.uk and I will hold you to account, or provide additional resources for you to achieve them.

If you let me have your address, I will send you your own Goals notepad, or you can pop to your local stationery store and pick one up. It will be the best investment you have ever made. Write your goals down. The next day, write them down again without referring to the ones written previously. Do this again the next day, and the next. The really important goals, just like cream, will rise to the top.

Have a really super life, I hope all your Goals Do Come True!

Your Goals List

1.

2.

3.

4.

5.

6.

7.

8.

9.

10.

About the Author

Doug Bennett is happily married to his wife Bonnie and has two amazing children, Jason and Jake.

Doug has been in financial services for nearly 40 years, starting out with the Halifax in the early 1980s, before engaging in a number of partnerships over the years. It was in 2006 that he decided the only person he could rely on was himself, and he set up DB Financial with his wife as an administrator.

In late 2019 he sold a proportion of his wealth planning business for a significant sum of money, which has enabled him to complete a number of his goals. It also gave him time to write this, his first book. Doug has spoken at a number of conferences globally, and plans to share his message to a much larger audience now he has more time available.

He is Chair of the Board of Trustees for a small local charity, Us in a Bus, where he has previously raised funds by running a half marathon and trekking up Kilimanjaro. He now sits on the board helping to direct the charity in its efforts to connect with severely handicapped and autistic adults.

Having had a couple of financial near misses during his life, as well as meandering through financial crises in the early '90s and the GFC in 2008, Doug has developed a very pragmatic attitude to life, has a wickedly dry sense of humour, and will help anyone.

More than a couple of people have said he is a lovely guy, so it must be true!

Printed in Great Britain
by Amazon